Whether you are in the midst of your own healing journey or providing care to someone who is, *Coaching and Healing* will give you fresh and powerful ways to understand healing at a deep level. The intimate personal narratives of ten incredibly generous and embodied Integral Master Coaches™ and the examples of their client work will hit you in the gut and leave you wanting to apply every word to your own life. May *Coaching and Healing* be of service as we each take steps, one after the other, on our own personal paths of wellness.

—Laura Divine and Joanne Hunt,
Co-Founders, Integral Coaching Canada, Inc.

The book *Coaching and Healing* pioneers a new area of research and practice, namely, the application of Integral Coaching to the process of healing. It's a natural match in many ways, and yet remains sadly under-applied at this time. *Coaching and Healing* aims to redress that lack by directly approaching the topic through the lens of Integral Theory and Integral Coaching itself. Although the book can be approached without any prior knowledge, it will likely be of more benefit to those familiar with either Integral Theory or Integral Coaching. But in any event, it demonstrates the clear importance and profound effectiveness of taking a more integral approach to the whole process of illness and healing.

—Ken Wilber
Author of *Integral Meditation* and *Integral Spirituality*

In *Coaching and Healing*, Dr. Joel Kreisberg and his colleagues describe a new model of patient care that is rapidly evolving, which is based on an integral perspective — attention not just to the physical aspects of a client but also his or her psychological, social, and spiritual needs. This coaching model evokes a patient's intrinsic wisdom through participation in narrative and self-exploration. In this process, healing becomes as important as curing, and the therapeutic results are often deeper and more enduring than in conventional therapeutic interchanges. This approach should be part of the skill set of anyone involved in patient care.

—Larry Dossey, MD
Executive Editor: *Explore:The Journal of Science and Healing*
Author of *One Mind* and *Reinventing Medicine*

The encounter with serious illness can either enclose our world in the suffering of "something's wrong," or become a portal for healing our heart and spirit. In this powerfully rendered, honest, and deeply wise book, the authors guide coaches in establishing the kind of coaching relationships that transcend the fixation on cures, and serve the deepest domain of healing and realizing inner freedom.

—Tara Brach PhD
Author of *Radical Accepta*nce and *True Refuge*

I was touched by the authors' heartfelt stories of their own healing journeys and their keen insights and questions related to coaching in health care. In their quest to bring together ten voices across two fields, they mirror the challenges both of them face. Rather than provide pat answers, they stand in the midst of the fray and offer some new starting points for dialogue and healing.

—David Drake, PhD
Director, Center for Narrative Coaching & Design

This book is a series of heartfelt inquiries into the perplexing landscapes human beings encounter when they shift from illness narratives to healing ones. The sensitivity of the authors to their clients and their candor about their own illness challenges make this book both an inspiring and illuminating read.

—Greg Jemsek
Narrative Therapist

This wise book, whose primary audience is health coaches, is chock full of insights into the facilitation of healing. Coming from Master Coaches trained in the Integral Coaching Canada model, the book flows freely from first-, second-, and third-person perspectives. As a physician, I realize that all health caregivers inevitably employ coaching techniques in practice, even if not primarily identifying as coaches. Accordingly, I strongly recommend this easily-read book to such caregivers as an introduction to effective techniques of healing and restoration.

—Gary Huffaker, MD

Some illnesses are hard to cure, with painful or chronic symptoms that can be tough to cope with. Healing is different. By exploring my own healing narrative, I realized that my chronic symptoms weren't because I had failed to cure myself. Instead they are a message from my own body and soul — a message helping me to find a different and happier way to live in the world. The Coaching and Healing process has changed my relationship with myself.

—Jason MacNaughton
Health and Wellness Client

This guide to *Coaching and Healing* is a practical textbook that contains profound potential within its pages. The narratives and practices provided here lead coaches and consultants to the very edge of their own beliefs and limitations while expanding their capacities to become true integral healers. This is the wisdom that will change lives, one at a time, and in so doing, will change our entire planet as well. I highly recommend *Coaching and Healing* to anyone who desires to practice in the liminal field where true healing occurs.

—Karen Wyatt MD
Author of *What Really Matters*

This book is a river of healing. Drink deeply of the compassionate wisdom, practical insights, and the soulful narratives that flow from these pages. It will only sensitize, strengthen, and ground your impact with those you touch through the healing practice of coaching.

—Barrett C. Brown, PhD
Managing Director, Apheno Advisory

This seminal book is of great benefit for health professionals, patients, and all individuals who wish to live life to the fullest extent. We have the ability to alter our perceptions of problems that arise, be they health issues, a loss, or a seemingly insurmountable stressful situation. *Coaching and Healing* is an excellent guide which describes the basis of the healing process and serves as an excellent guide to a greater sense of well-being and fulfillment.

—Len Wisneski, MD, FACP

It is perhaps no accident that Reggie Marra is a poet as well as a healing coach. The moving narratives he and his colleagues have chosen for this book reflect a poet's thinking, that is, a creative vision of what healing is beyond the rigid medical conventions. The authors put forth two categories, *pathogenesis*, which reflects the traditional medical idea of disease and curing, and *salutogenesis*, which literally means "the creation of health or the fostering of healing." It is this latter category with which a healing coach is most concerned. This book presents a bright new window on how to approach what we all face as human beings with a body.

—Doug Anderson
Author, *Horse Medicine* and *Keep Your Head Down: A Memoir –
Vietnam, the Sixties, and a Journey of Self-Discovery*

In my 2 decades of experience as a western trained allopathic physician I have witnessed how our healthcare system, much like our other social systems (such as our education and judicial structures), has increasingly become constrained by a worldview that is no longer sustainable. A worldview that supports a reductionist and mechanistic way of engaging the world, which naturally gravitates to approaching health and wellness through the lens of what the authors of *Coaching and Healing* call the pathogenic model. In my view, their description of a salutogenic model that emphasizes healing narrative is a critical next step in the evolution of what medicine and our health care system could become. The approach to health articulated in this prescient book is the natural consequence of the growth in individual and societal conscience that is predicted by Ken Wilber's Integral vision.

—Rajvir Dhillon, MD

This volume is about the richness of coaching and how coaches augment their clients' capacity to address healing. Coaches have the ability to consider their clients both through their own perspective and, in a deeply empathic stance, through the clients' own eyes and experience. Kreisberg, et al. ask the coach to develop the skill of being "inside" the client — feeling what he or she feels, seeing the world from his or her perspective. To do this, coaches must inquire into their own healing resources to recognize and relate to the varying circumstances and motivations of our clients — getting clear on what is ours and what is theirs. Kreisberg, et al. lay out a series of coaching sessions that offers great opportunity for accomplishing what they intend. They lay out how coaches can help their clients shift from a disease narrative to a healing narrative. The case stories from coaches augment this writing and add greater depth and detail to the process. I highly recommend this book as a healing narrative and an illustration of what can be accomplished when human beings put their minds together for healing purposes.

—Lewis Mehl-Madrona, MD, PhD
Coyote Institute for Studies of Change and Transformation
Author of *Coyote Medicine* and *Narrative Medicine*

Coaching and Healing offers us a comprehensive approach to critical health and wellness issues that affect us all. This insightful book asks us to reflect on our beliefs around pain and disease, and then shows us how we can take appropriate coaching steps toward healing. It combines heartfelt stories with practical pathways to help us navigate the journey through injury, illness, trauma or loss. The authors walk this intimate path with the reader throughout the book, sharing their personal hopes, fears, and coaching lessons learned along the way. These pragmatic teachings enable us to see what beliefs, habits, living and work environments, and/or relationships may be promoting or thwarting our wellness. Having served as a military officer in Iraq and Afghanistan, I know that reading this work will lift your spirits as you discover healthy alternatives to pain and suffering.

—Fred Krawchuk, U.S. Army Colonel (retired)
Strategic Advisor, Coming Home Project,
dedicated to healing the trauma of war

After 20 years of being witness to thousands of healings and transformations in people, I have observed that there are some keystones that support true change. Peace of mind, surrender to what is and feeling safe physically and emotionally play a vital role in accessing the intelligence that resides within us all to heal, grow and create.

They say you can never leave somewhere that you have never been. How true. For anyone to deeply acknowledge their story, the unfolding of their life, and honor it for both the challenges and the gifts it brings, is powerful. In a sense it alters the perspective held regarding any situation, particularly those relating to a health crisis, as ON the way versus IN the way. How comforting to view the various trials of life as stepping stones to growth instead of cohorts to destruction.

The authors of *Coaching and Healing* bring an incredible depth of personal experience and the understanding of salutogenic healing. The real life examples of the transformations stewarded through their approach are thought provoking and inspirational.

Ultimately, healing is an inside job. Narrative healing is a key that can unlock the door allowing the innate expression of our health potential to come out and play.

—Richard Yoshimura, DC

A fascinating read for anyone who wants to tap into intrinsic healing power, supported by integral coaching and holistic, complementary medicine. The authors are salutogenic heroes whose collaboration fosters a much-needed transformation of health care.

—Meg Jordan, PhD, RN, CWP
Co-President, National Wellness Institute

COACHING
and HEALING

COACHING
and HEALING

Transcending the Illness Narrative

JOEL KREISBERG, ALEX DOUDS, AMY PHILLIPS,
JILL LANG WARD, JOHN STODDART,
JULIE FLAHERTY, KARIN HEMPEL,
LESLIE WILLIAMS, LOIS MACNAUGHTON,
REGGIE MARRA

Copyright 2016 Integral Publishers

Integral Publishers
4845 E. 2nd Street
Tucson, AZ 85711
831-333-9200

ISBN: 978-1-4951-8771-1

Cover and Interior Design by Kathryn Lloyd

DEDICATION

To our common humanity and all beings — each of us and all of us,
known and not known, as together we suffer, learn, teach,
heal, and encourage healing.

And in memory of our colleague
and dear friend, Jill Lang Ward,
who healed, and encouraged healing.
July 31, 1952 – May 26, 2016

LIKE YOU

by Roque Dalton, translated by Jack Hirschman

Like you I
love love, life, the sweet smell
of things, the sky-blue
landscape of January days.

And my blood boils up
and I laugh through eyes
that have known the buds of tears.

I believe the world is beautiful
and that poetry, like bread, is for everyone.

And that my veins don't end in me
but in the unanimous blood
of those who struggle for life,
love,
little things,
landscape and bread,
the poetry of everyone.

TABLE OF CONTENTS

PREFACE

In what ways can we be of greater service in the relief of suffering? What initiatives might we enact to bring our ideas and our gifts into the world with more power and grace? How can we move from a personal to a global perspective? Integral Coaching® founders, Laura Divine and Joanne Hunt, planted the seeds for this book when they posed these questions at our 2012 Mastery Workshop in Ottawa, Canada.

Inspired by this call to action, a group of coaches formed with a collective desire to explore the role that coaching can play in healing. We wondered how we could deepen, strengthen, and hone what seemed a natural connection between coaching and healing in our own lives and in our coaching practices. We were also curious about a bigger picture. What could we offer our fellow coaches around the world? And how could we contribute to the broader conversation about health coaching as it emerges, a vital new modality within the healing arts and sciences?

Coaching and Healing is the product of our remarkable collaboration—ten coaches from across North America, meeting monthly, online, over four years. At the outset, we realized how much we enjoyed simply coming together with our shared purpose, many of us with profound experiences with health challenges, many with equally profound experiences with healing, and as healers. Supported by our varied backgrounds in business and organizational leadership, project management, education, writing, medicine, and law, we forged a dynamic, heartfelt and resilient alliance.

We opened our meetings with poetry. Reggie Marra, with life-affirming authority, selected and read each poem, then guided us through a few minutes of free writing and free sharing. Surprised and delighted by our discoveries, we would sink together into the world of the poem, our vulnerabilities stirred and our attentions sharpened. Poetry helped us shift our highly personal experiences into the universal, and that connectedness informed each step of our work. First proposing that we write a paper for our coaching colleagues, Joel Kreisberg defined and focused our energies and our goals. From that initial paper, through presentations, and finally this book, Joel provided the compass points and driving force to move our project ever onward.

We hope *Coaching and Healing* will reach and serve coaches of all stripes, along with their clients. We wish to give physicians, health care practitioners and their patients, an intimate understanding of the power of coaching to support treatment and help chart a healing path through illness. And for everyone in the fields of health and wellness, in care homes and hospices, even teachers and students of life-writing, we offer this book as a testament to the spark of transformation residing within each of us.

In addition to those mentioned above we acknowledge our editor, Tim Owens. It is unusual for a book to have ten authors. Our voices have joined together, as those in a choir, and as such we offer our deepest gratitude to one another. May we all be well.

—John Stoddart
Ottawa, Canada, Spring 2016

Our colleague John Stoddart wrote the words "Coaching and Healing" atop one of a dozen or so blank posters hanging from a conference room wall back in April 2012. Nine of us chose to join him to explore this topic – not knowing where we might go together. Thank you, John.

HEALING IS MANY THINGS

—John Stoddart

What is healing? This question is my compass as I navigate the wild territory of illness. Perhaps what is most fascinating and unfathomable about healing is that we are drawn to simple solutions, when in fact everyone's experience of healing is utterly unique and rarely straightforward. No single thing brings about healing because healing is so many, many things.

LEAPING INTO SURRENDER

—Karin Hempel

Sixty feet in the air and the ground seemed so close and so hard. All I had to do was jump—how difficult could it be? Mind you, I was completely tethered and being held by trusted companions. Yet at that moment, after exhausting all options of how to get off the diving board attached to the tree while maintaining my dignity, I still couldn't bring myself to make the leap.

Eventually, I surrendered to what was sure to be my inevitable death. I thought, "If I'm going to die, I might as well make it spectacular." I gathered my courage, hoped for the best, and flung myself into empty air with all the dramatics of a high diver. The rope caught me mid-leap and I was gently lowered to the ground. I was instantly surrounded by friends and congratulated on my bravery.

Years later, when I found out that my breast cancer had metastasized to my spine, I would again have the opportunity to surrender and I did— what choice did I have? That was when true healing began.

For most of my life I have been incredibly healthy and very active. Aside from an appendectomy, I had no other health complaints in my first four decades. In 2006, I was told that I had breast cancer, the diagnosis that rocked me to my core. At the time, I was in the midst of studying for my Master's degree in Holistic Health Education. Ironic. And yet, my passion for a broader understanding of health served me well as I undertook to battle this disease.

I opted for surgery—no radiation or chemo. I believed that my understanding of nutrition and healthy lifestyle would ensure that the cancer didn't return. And I was right ... for about two years.

When the cancer returned, with the additional diagnosis of metastasis, I was again rocked to my core. I began to have doubts about what I had learned. I wondered if chemotherapy and radiation might really be the only ways to ensure cancer didn't come back, and I was scared—deeply scared. The stories of the pain and suffering people go through with cancer are easily accessible on the Internet. I was advised to undergo a radical mastectomy with reconstructive surgery. Much of what I thought made me a woman was about to be removed—and not in an easy way.

Standing in front of the mirror in a hotel where my husband and I were staying while meeting with my California-based oncologists and surgeons, I looked at myself in lacy black underwear and said, "Well, at least I'll still have a breast even if it isn't real." In that moment, I surrendered to whatever was going to happen. What other choice did I have? I had no other options. The biggest decision I needed to make was whether I would do the surgery in California, where my family and friends lived, or Colorado, my new home where I knew very few people. We went back to Colorado to make our decision. Then the miracles started occurring.

I was fortunate enough to work with someone who volunteered with organizations that supported cancer research. I asked him to help me find someone good. I ended up with the most respected oncologist in the state of Colorado, whose specialty was cancer of the breast and in the bone. My husband and I sat before him as though we were about to go to the gallows. All I wanted to know was whether it was going to be the chemo first, then the surgery, then the radiation, or surgery first and then the chemo and radiation. The answer was—none of the above. The doctor prescribed Tamoxifen and a bone strengthener once a month.

At about the same time, I had met a homeopath who put me onto a protocol developed specifically for cancer that was called "plussing." I began the protocol and the pain in my back and spine due to the metastasis went away immediately and completely.

I had a friend who knew of a naturopathic oncologist in Oregon whose focus was prescribing herbs and supplements to naturally support the body in healing in conjunction with Western protocols. I'd also heard of an energy healer who had great results with cancer patients. Ever the skeptic, I decided to at least give it a try.

Today I am living with cancer. The good news is it's going away. The healing journey began when I surrendered and continued through the usage of homeopathy to take away the bone pain and reduce the cancer, to the Western doctor's prescription to take Tamoxifen and a bone strengthener, to the life-supporting recommendations of the naturopathic oncologist, to the utterly mind-blowing changes I've experienced using an energy healer. The result has been nothing short of miraculous.

This journey has not been easy. It has required me to be fully engaged. It has required me to surrender my notion of what works and to surrender my ego and let go of beliefs and emotions that don't serve me. I have had to accept the fact that there are people who love and support me, who want me to be well. I have been forced to surrender the belief that I will live forever. And that's okay, too.

Cancer has given me the greatest gift. I have learned to live in the "now," to follow my truth, to go deep into my emotional and spiritual space and see unpleasant things, heal them, and move on. The depth of emotional and spiritual change I have experienced on this journey eclipses any physical changes. My life is rich, full, happy, and wonderful.

Surrender used to feel like such a weak thing to do. Yet, in my experience, once it happens, a whole new world opens up, a world you never dreamed possible. Author Richard Roll said, "Surrender is letting go... it's trust to the hundredth power—not sticking to your idea of the outcome, but letting go in the faith that even the absence of an outcome will be the perfect solution."

Give it a try. You'll be amazed at the healing that can take place.

INTRODUCTION

Healing is a transformation of view rather than a cure. It involves recognizing your intrinsic wholeness and, simultaneously, your connectedness to everything else. Above all it involves coming to feel at peace within yourself.

—Jon Kabat-Zinn

The authors, all trained and certified as Integral Master Coaches through Integral Coaching Canada, Inc. (ICC), have engaged in a several-year journey to better understand healing from the inside. This guide to coaching and healing is a gathering of our collective wisdom and experience of coaching when healing from injury, illness, or trauma is central to the coaching program. We have drawn from both our experiences in coaching clients through the healing process and our own personal healing journeys.

Two approaches to healing are considered: *pathogenic*, the dominant biomedical model which focuses on diagnosis and treatment of disease; and *salutogenic*, which models healing as a continuum that includes both illness and wellness, focusing on the creation of health on that continuum. We accept both models and choose to engage the more potent opportunity by emphasizing the salutogenic or health-creating approach.

An essential aspect of our group's process involved the creation of personal healing narratives, highlighting the unique resources we each engaged during our individual healing processes. These healing narratives are interspersed throughout this book, offering examples of the diversity of healing stories that can take place during the healing journey. Over time, we have come to integrate healing narratives into our coaching programs as an essential tool for helping clients understand themselves better, as well as become more familiar with their own skills that are engaged when healing occurs.

While the authors' shared coach training and method, as it is applied to healing, informs this book, we emphasize *specific, essential qualities of the coaching relationship*, not tied to any method, which support clients through their healing. For clarity, this is followed by a step-by-step analysis of our shared method. We then include excerpts from real-life coaching sessions that exemplify some of the specific approaches used in coaching for healing. Our hope is that all coaches who are committed to healing will benefit from our work.

In Chapter One, "Including Both Perspectives in Coaching," we offer a foundation in the language of *illness, healing,* and *curing* as it applies to the coaching relationship. More specifically, we differentiate *illness* narratives and *healing* narratives and clarify the difference between *healing* and *curing* within the respective views of *pathogenesis* and *salutogenesis*. With this foundation in place, we explore our experiences of the unique challenges that coaches face when coaching in a healing context.

In Chapter Two, "Working With Healing Narratives," we offer the nuts and bolts of the healing narrative—what it is, how coaches can support clients in writing their narratives, specific exercises and practices that the authors have used, and engaging poetry and poetry writing as a healing practice.

Chapter Three, "The Four Stages of the Integral Coaching Journey," provides an overview of the four types of conversations that are used in ICC's Integral Coaching method with a specific focus on these conversations within a healing context. The chapter follows an actual case study through the intake, offer, cycle of development, and completion conversations.

Chapter Four, "Case Studies," offers five additional case studies from the authors that further clarify what is necessary and what is possible when coaching in a healing context. Each case is written in the coach's authentic voice and demonstrates the inevitably diverse unfoldings, even within the same coaching methodology, that unique coaches, clients, and topics bring to this work.

Chapter Five, "Moving Forward," brings us to next steps for coaches who work with clients in areas that call for healing. Based on the lessons the authors have learned and are still learning, we deeply believe that coaches who work with clients amid any forms of illness, disease, injury, loss, or grief need to deepen their own relationships with loss and healing. Chapter Five offers three ways to do this.

FINISHING WELL ...

—Jill Lang-Ward

My healing journey began in 2007 when I was diagnosed with stage III multiple myeloma, a rare, incurable but treatable cancer of plasma cells in the bone marrow. Suddenly, my world was turned upside down! I had just turned 55 and was about to retire. Engaging in a battle with cancer was not how I had envisioned retirement.

Within three months I retired and began the fight for my life. Living with cancer became my new "career." As author and survivor Kris Carr says, "You have a full-time job—you are always at the office of healing." How very true.

Being told you have a terminal illness completely rocks your world. Yet, the truth is, life is terminal, and we each have the opportunity to choose how we want to live the precious life we are given. For me, that has been cancer's greatest gift.

I embraced my illness wholeheartedly, knowing that there was a Divine purpose in all of this. I was determined from the outset to share my experience as a service to others in their personal healing journeys. This has been very rewarding and brought me so much joy.

The past eight years have been a roller coaster ride. Having experienced a successful autologous stem cell transplant followed by three years of complete remission, then two relapses (disappointing but not unexpected), I continue to do well thanks to new therapies that are helping me kick cancer's butt.

In 2013, my cancer treatment was interrupted due to diverticular disease that resulted in four hospitalizations for serious bowel obstructions, E. coli infections and ultimately, colostomy surgery. During that time I faced my mortality twice. Because I had virtually no immune system, medical staff were amazed that I survived. Yet I did! I believe it was Divine intervention once again. During many hours spent in the hospital, deep breathing and meditation became my best ally, getting me through some very difficult times.

Following my second relapse, cytogenetics testing identified a specific gene abnormality that placed me in a higher risk category for a poorer prognosis. According to current statistics, I have surpassed my life expectancy—and I keep beating the odds! As I write this my myeloma count is lower than it's been in seven years, and my doctors are amazed and puzzled.

I am deeply grateful to my incredible health care team who take such good care of me as I continue my journey. I have never felt more loved as I am surrounded and held by the loving support of so many friends, family, and fellow travelers along this wild and wonderful Path.

My illness has strengthened me and brought me many unexpected gifts that have hugely contributed to my healing.

I have found meaning and purpose in my life. I am more attuned to what really matters. I appreciate each and every day. Accepting impermanence awakened me to the truth that I have actually been afraid to truly live. Now, I am living more fully than ever.

Living with cancer created a wealth of new opportunities to support others in similar circumstances. I enjoy my weekly visits to the chemo suite and have developed many new friendships with other "chemo-sabies." At the same time, I have lost many fellow warriors and that has been painful. It has, however, been a privilege to accompany them and learn from their experiences facing the end of life.

While I am not afraid of death, I have come to realize that I have had difficulty with completion in many aspects of my life. Perhaps that is why Finishing Well has become my last and most important big project. I am currently writing my story ... Finishing Well is the title of the first chapter.

There is no question that traditional chemotherapy treatments have helped to keep me alive, and for that I am exceedingly grateful. My strong faith and "still breathing" meditation practice continues to serve me well in my healing journey. I also believe there is a higher power working through me, and my purpose here is not yet fulfilled. Whispers tell me I still have lots more to do. As long as I am still breathing, I will carry on.

I believe that we each have the power to heal ourselves. I also believe that Love is healing, and with Love ALL things are possible. In my experience, when you give Love it comes back tenfold. What could be more healing than that?

One big lesson I have learned is the importance—in fact the necessity—of self-love and compassion. This is a work in progress for me.

I continue to learn to let go and trust that things will work out the way they are intended. Each night I repeat Louise Hay's affirmation, "All is well and I am safe." When I do so, I relax and just breathe; it feels liberating and prepares me for a peaceful sleep. Upon waking in the morning, I hug my precious Border Collie saying, "God's given us another day to play, Brodie. How shall we spend it?" And my mysterious journey continues ...

The biggest lessons that my illness has taught me are:
- *Our gift is in our pain.*
- *I've only regretted the things I didn't do.*
- *I need to be kind, compassionate and more gentle with myself so that I can more fully love others.*
- *Accepting "what is" is liberating.*

If I were to offer advice to someone on a healing journey ...
- *Do what you want while you can!*
- *Live your own life—it's way more fun!*

- *Never ever give up Hope!*
- *For unconditional love ... become an Integral Coach ... or, even better, get a dog!*

∞

Chapter 1

Perspectives on Healing in Coaching

Healing may not be so much about getting better, as about letting go of everything that isn't you—all of the expectations, all of the beliefs—and becoming who you are.

—Rachel Naomi Remen

Whatever you resist; persists. The healing route is the opposite of resistance, it is acceptance. The way out is the way through, to open up, release our feelings, accept and let them go. To face reality as it is, which is much easier with love in our hearts rather than negative interpretations and self-defeating beliefs.

—Peter Shepherd

Illness versus Healing

How do we know we are healing? What starts us healing and how does it grow? Is this just the opposite of getting sick? Clients often have little understanding of the skills and mechanics of healing. They come to coaches with a focus on removing the causes of their disease. Our medical system has evolved emphasizing the rational origins of illness and disease. *Pathogenesis* describes the creation and development of disease. Healing is tacitly accepted as the removing of pathogenic stimuli. Yet in the late 20th century, our understanding grew to include the biopsychosocial factors for illness, which broadened our perspective to include broader influences including psychological, social, and environmental. An Israeli sociologist, Aaron Antonovsky, researched and articulated a counterpart to pathogenesis, calling this process, *salutogenesis*, which literally means the creation of health or the fostering of healing. *Saluto* (health) *genesis* (origins) emphasizes healing and health-promoting behaviors, which have a significantly different orientation than the removal of the causes of illness.

The Health-ease/Dis-ease Continuum, the initial context for Antovovsky's model, emphasizes the complete spectrum of health, disease, and healing. It essentially appears in the more familiar *Illness-Wellness Continuum or the Wellness Paradigm* developed by John Travis (2004), a key feature of health coaching. The *Illness-Wellness Continuum* considers both the progression of the symptoms of illness and the health-generating changes towards wellness. Healing, as we use it in this book, includes both the reduction of symptoms, improvement of health, and the process by which we move towards the healthy end of the Illness-Wellness Continuum. No matter where one starts on the continuum, from a serious episode of chronic illness or a simple desire to lose weight, the stages of healing can be learned and enhanced. A truly integrative approach will therefore include the entire spectrum of healing, including reduction of the causes of illness or trauma and the enhancement of healing through salutogenic development.

What are the factors that move one toward the more salutary end of the continuum? These factors include a) cognitive appraisal, gaining a full understanding of the nature of the illness and the necessary steps required for healing to occur; b) increased coping mechanisms, becoming more skilled and resilient about managing stressors; c) improved host resistance, the ability of the organism to recognize challenges to its integrity and maintain homeostasis; d) improved adaptive response, increased tolerance of a wider range of reactivity; and, finally, e) a stronger *Sense of Coherence* (SOC), the model Antonovsky researched and developed as the key element in *salutogenesis.*

A *Sense of Coherence* (SOC) is "the global orientation that expresses the extent to which an individual has a pervasive, enduring, dynamic feeling of confidence that one's internal and external environments are predictable and that there is a high probability that things will work out as well as can reasonably be expected" (Antonovsky, 1979, p. 126). Enhancing such an orientation offers a powerful goal for coaching and healing. The Sense of Coherence model orients around three primary foci:

- *Comprehensibility* – the extent to which both internal or psychological stimuli and external or environmental stimuli make sense.
- *Manageability* – the extent to which available resources are adequate.
- *Meaningfulness* – the extent to which challenging events are seen as worthy of being engaged emotionally (Levin, 2008).

In coaching and healing, the coach seeks to reinforce comprehension and manageability while enhancing meaningfulness. By increasing participation, motivation and emotional investment, clients gain control of their circumstance and increasingly shape a positive outcome.

One way we learn to heal is through successfully managing stress. The salutogenic model accepts mild to moderate stressors as common, ongoing experiences that create repeated tensions within us. Rather than focusing on reducing stressors or stress, we mobilize internal resources in an effort to alleviate the impact of these stressors. By intentionally and repeatedly attending to this salutogenic process, we are better able to overcome the impact of disease factors and return to health.

Over time, we can certainly develop improved coping responses which allow us to modify situations, better control stress, and engage meaningfully in the these situations. Coaching, as differentiated from conventional medicine, can utilize these coping responses to support positive change, increase healing resources, and lessen physical, emotional, and mental illness, increasing wellness.

THE DIFFERENCE BETWEEN ILLNESS AND DISEASE

—John Stoddart

We use these two words to mean the same thing, yet there is a vital distinction to be made. Disease is the label, what your doctor diagnoses and treats. Illness is your experience, your relationship with the disease. As Dr. E. J. Cassell puts it, illness is "what the patient feels when he goes to the doctor" and disease is "what he has on the way home."

With disease, we strive to be objective, just the provable, measurable facts. With illness, we cannot help but be subjective. Through illness we manifest our beliefs and feelings and express our deepest selves. When I was young, I had a recurring dream of desperately clinging to the edge of a cliff by my fingertips. Without the strength to pull myself up, I drew upon my willpower to hold on just a little longer, longer, longer. This vision became my real life story of illness. From the age of fifteen, for over forty years, an evolving and compounding constellation of progressive symptoms led eventually to mental and physical collapse. At no time, despite valiant effort, did I receive a comprehensive diagnosis or viable treatment. Along with my health, I lost my job, career, income, savings, spouse, and home. Faced with such extreme loss I came to believe that no matter what I did life was going to continue to drain away, and whatever energy I might summon would certainly not last. Yet I continued to cling, ever willful, to my metaphoric cliff.

Long after I gave up hope of an explanation or a path to wellness, a diagnosis was offered: chronic Lyme disease. Decades of mystery began to make sense. Treatment brought incremental shifts in symptoms, then measurable improvement. For the first time in my adult life I was now healing rather than sickening. Paradoxically, the medical field is split on the question of whether or not there is such a disease as chronic Lyme. Nevertheless, diagnosis brought critical parts of my illness into perspective and helped lift me from the cliff edge.

Engaging my power to heal means updating my story from one of sickening to one of healing. Two people, even with the same disease, will each have their own very personal stories that are shaped by the questions that illness elicits. What's happening to me? Why? Why now? What do I do about it? You need to answer these, but you don't have to do it alone. To understand how our beliefs and behaviors shape our experience of illness, we need to tap into our own inherent wisdom, gather lots of support, listen to other's interpretations, and collect objective data. This is where Integral Coaching can be life-changing. Together, we navigate the subjective and objective aspects of your world. My experience of illness becomes my door to healing.

SHIFTING THE NARRATIVE: FROM CURING TO HEALING

Learning to attend to the experience of healing is critical. The process of creating a healing narrative encourages increased access to resources that heal by bringing attention to past healing experiences and the salutogenic processes involved. The significance of narrative healing has grown over the past 30 years, beginning with the seminal work of Arthur Kleinman (1989) and James Pennebaker (1990) followed by Rita Charon (2009) and Lewis Mehl-Madrona (2007). While Kleinman and Charon's works have mostly focused on the illness narrative, Mehl-Madrona and others have proffered healing stories that emerge naturally as perspectives broaden to include the movement towards wellness. These salutogenic experiences explore meaning beyond the story of getting sick, placing the emphasis on healing rather than illness. In a coaching setting, developing a healing narrative offers a significant opportunity to engage the client in framing experiences that include, enhance, and strengthen positive resources.

WAYS OF SEEING THAT BLOCK THE HEALING PROCESS

As coaches, we consider how a client might be open, closed, or limited in their capacity to address healing. Individuals with similar circumstances may see themselves as competent travelers with potential for growth or as hopeless victims limited by mortal bodies and poorly resourced circumstances. Certain common patterns shape our relationship to suffering and may open or close our capacity to experience healing and health. Do we relate to our illness as something outside ourselves or as an aspect of who we are? As coaches we have the ability to consider our clients both through our own perspective and, in a deeply empathic stance, consider what the world looks like through *their* eyes and experience. The conventional approach is one in which we consider the strengths and weaknesses of our clients, assessing life skills and potentials for growth. In this way we are looking *at* our clients rather than understanding them from the inside.

Looking *as* the client offers a subjective and compassionate approach that asks the coach to develop the skill of being "inside" the client—feeling what he or she feels, seeing the world from his or her perspective. To better do this, we must take the necessary steps of inquiring into our own healing resources. In this way we are better able to recognize and relate to the varying circumstances and motivations of our clients—getting clear on what is ours and what is theirs. This inquiry is modeled throughout this book, with each author sharing his or her own experience of healing through the development of the healing narrative.

Often, stressors are perceived as negative or causes of illness. In the salutogenic approach to coaching, stressors are less the focus, though the beliefs that emerge from chronic stressors can be essential to examine. Noted author and physician Gabor Maté (2009), offers the following perspective on the impact of stressors and our beliefs:

> *We have seen that stress is a result of interaction between a stressor and a processing system. That processing apparatus is the*

human nervous system, operating under the influence of the brain's emotional center. The biology of belief inculcated in that processing apparatus early in life crucially influences our stress responses throughout our lives. Do we recognize stressors? Do we minimize or maximize potential threats to our wellbeing? Do we perceive ourselves as alone? As never needing help? As having to work to deserve love? As hopelessly unlovable? These are unconscious beliefs embedded at the cellular level. They control our behavior no matter what we may think at the conscious level. They keep us in shut-down mode or allow us to open to growth and to health.

Some of these beliefs are illustrated below:

As we become more attuned with our own beliefs, we build a felt sense of experiences that will allow us to serve our clients in engaging new opportunities for removing blockages. Our way of seeing our clients can shift from "helping" them reduce or remove stressors, to deepening their understanding of their own innate beliefs and healing resources. Rather than overcoming stressors alone, our work is in strengthening resources by better understanding our own and our clients' limiting beliefs. Through empathy and acknowledgment, we offer potential for dissolving blockages that prevent our clients and ourselves from taking the necessary actions that nurture healing. Increasing our familiarity with the beliefs that bind and the resources that motivate strengthens the coach's and the client's abilities to activate the healing response.

THE COACHING RELATIONSHIP: DISTINCTIONS FOR HEALING

Healing is a spontaneous event that comes about through a kind of grace. It can happen anytime, and in anyplace. It may come about simply with a smile from a stranger, the breeze blowing through the trees, the singing of a bird—some reminder of our connectedness and wholeness—the beauty of life just as it is at this moment for us.

—Mary Maddox

Coaching in a healing context presents a unique challenge. This is evident when we acknowledge that healing from illness and loss tends to be a universal challenge for all of us, coach and client. Here are some examples, just from our own experience:

- A good friend lost her brother to suicide a few years ago. Her healing from the loss has been slow as she continuously questions what happened, why it happened, and whether she could have done something about it.
- A best friend has gone through two bouts of colon cancer with small odds for survival, according to available statistics, and doesn't like to talk about it.
- A coaching client whose wife died of cancer two years ago has been unable to change anything in the house because it would dishonor her.
- An uncle is expressing anger and sadness at having to leave his home for an assisted living facility at the age of 90.
- A client seeking coaching shortly after her husband had a severe stroke is living with the uncertainty about how to support him and their future.
- A client with chronic pain for 20 years wants to wake up in the morning with a greater sense of purpose in her life.

The common thread through each of these stories is the experience of loss—losing physical capacity, a loved family member, the security of home, a sense of purpose—and its impact on our sense of wellbeing. Experiences of loss are universal, and the potential for healing considerable as we continue to engage in life.

This territory is very rich, often in shadow, hidden from our awareness, and ripe with potential for growth. "Illness" is used here in three ways: as shorthand for a client's unique expression of suffering; as an aspect of identity; and as a way of being. Where loss has occurred, coaches are working in especially vulnerable terrain. One of the salient aspects of working with loss is how this affects the coach, who must be attuned to the subtler dynamics of feelings connected with loss. Not only must we bring the same set of skills as in any other coaching circumstance, we also need to apply even greater sensitivity and skill. Hurt needs tender care.

All coaching engages some degree of vulnerability in our clients. In coaching and healing existential questions are closer to the surface; pain and suffering are often also close at hand. Thus coaching involves high levels of compassion, flexibility, and the ability to attune to the client's world. In practical terms this means:

1. A coach working in the context of healing must embody an understanding of the potential sense of "groundlessness" that illness and loss create.

   Clients often experience some disorientation in the process of growth. It's a natural part of the process. Losing one's health can also be deeply disorienting. It can profoundly disrupt core questions of identity and place in the world, what actions are possible or desirable within this state of dis-ease, and what outcomes can be hoped for—essential elements of an intentionally lived life. In the face of illness, injury or other significant loss, clients can experience a deep disintegration, a sense of utter groundlessness.

   Though a challenging state, this loss of "myself—life as I know it" may also have tremendous transformative potential; it might be a sacred groundlessness. It demands that, as coaches, we remain calm in the face of strong symptoms and that we not move too quickly to focus the client on positive outcomes. Rather, we must directly understand the realities, pitfalls, and potential of mind or body disorganization and skillfully accompany our client in reorientation. Being able to compassionately walk with our client's experience, just as it is, allows a necessary space for healing.

2. The coach must shed inflated ambitions for the client to get better.

Healing does not necessarily mean curing. As coaches, we are called to resist over-emphasizing improvement of the client's condition (e.g. more energy, greater physical fitness, or an action plan for "getting rid" of the condition). With healing, we may be limited to qualitative goals such as an increased sense of peace, a greater ability to see beauty in the mundane, and even a deeper appreciation for the "new and different" potentials presented by current limitations.

Potentially, the coach's agenda for a client can be a real disservice. A healing context that emphasizes positive outcomes can accidentally send a deeply negating message to a client who may already be suffering shame, chronic pain, or both. Fixing the condition is not necessarily the required outcome of the coaching process and may inhibit a client's healing by overly focusing on quantifiable results.

We may need to adjust our expectations for how far or fast healing can occur. When energy is unpredictable or low or individuals have limited resources for accomplishing the most basic tasks of life, we often have to greatly reduce the scale or frequency of our practices, or adjust our frequency of visits.

Tiny shifts can sometimes catalyze major progress. Coaching and healing requires a compassionate heart, a patient body, and an especially keen awareness for subtle shifts and cues.

3. The coach must gauge not only the client's competency for healing, but also his or her capacity for healing in order to determine appropriate pace and scale of practices.

    As we use them here, *competency* refers to a level of skill in a given task or activity; *capacity* refers to the current access one has to that skill level. When working with healing, we must carefully attune to relevant *competencies*, as well as our client's *capacity*, or current ability, to access and engage them. Examples of competencies include physical competencies such as level of fitness, dexterity, and coordination, emotional competencies such as ability to recognize and express feelings, and mental competencies such as ability to stay focused or practice mindfulness. Illness or injury can fundamentally shift what's possible. Clients who naturally possess a high level of body-mind awareness and a strong ability to relate to their body as a source of wisdom, i.e., persons with high somatic *competency* — may suffer a physical condition that limits their *capacity* to engage in physical practices. In this, and any case, the client's competencies can only be engaged according to available capacity.

4. The coach must attune, even more keenly than usual, to the boundary between coaching and other healing disciplines.

    Regardless of a client's presenting issue, coaches must understand the limitations of their own knowledge and the boundaries in the coaching relationship. While engaging in coaching and healing, we are more likely to be working close to the borders of other disciplines such as conventional medicine, integrative medicine, or psychotherapy. It is much easier and less effective to separate clients from their medical practitioners than to complement current treatment protocols. When a client is physically or emotionally fragile, a misstep on our part can be disruptive, and monitoring our professional scope is essential. Coaching and healing require clarity about the limitations of the coaching process, seeking transparent management of the boundaries of the coaching role. Understanding and honoring the treatment protocols of our clients helps them feel a greater sense of coherence.

5. The coach must be sensitive to the client's grieving process in the face of loss.

When a client presents a healing topic it will frequently be linked to a felt sense of loss. It is necessary to tune into the emotional landscape of where the client might be in terms of the stages of grief or loss. The Kubler-Ross model, referred to as the five stages of grief, suggests that when we are faced with a loss we will experience a series of emotional stages, not always in sequence, and in our own unique way. The stages include denial, anger, bargaining, depression, and acceptance. Kubler-Ross originally applied these stages to people suffering from terminal illness. She later expanded her theoretical model to any form of catastrophic personal loss. Such losses may also include significant life events such as death of a loved one, major rejection, end of a relationship or divorce, the onset of a disease or chronic illness, as well as other tragedies and disasters. Her model provides an excellent foundation for understanding the structure of the experience our clients are seeking to heal. Awareness of these stages allows coaches a fuller understanding of this universal process, helping refine our approach in assessing and working with clients in the context of healing.

What This Means for Coaches

What capabilities does the coach need in order to create a healing environment? The ICC method, in which the authors were trained, requires that the coach embrace the following capabilities, allowing what is already present to be acknowledged and inviting what is possible.

ICC Integral Coaching Capabilities—What Already Is:

1. Sit openly/unconditionally with another human being, suspending our own judgments and defenses.
2. Observe with all our senses—heart, body, and mind.
3. Skillfully pose questions to shine the light on new areas in a client's world—objective and subjective.
4. Let the client's perspectives on the world form in front of us, to reveal that which is driving their action and words.
5. Combine rigor of assessment with intuitive formation (objective and subjective).

ICC Integral Coaching Capabilities—What is Possible:

1. Be still enough to sense what is emerging for the client in their words, wishes, and stories.
2. Sit with the bigger possibilities until what is essential emerges.
3. Hold the space.
4. Trust the "rigor and intuitive dance" such that we can hear the possibility.
5. Find language, metaphor, and/or story for what is emerging or envisioned (Hunt & Divine, 2004).

These capabilities, while necessary for all skilled coaching, are essential for setting the healing context. Due to the modern social and medical disposition that focuses on the illness narrative, the healing narrative is often ill-formed and unsupported. Considerable opportunity for emotional and spiritual growth occurs through the coaching conversation. The above-mentioned capabilities play a key role in shaping the healing narrative and the wellness focus of the coaching process. Because illness often has physical, mental, emotional, and spiritual aspects, the full presence of the coach is essential. The coach in whom these capabilities are embodied offers powerful potential for client healing and growth.

SUMMARY

Coaching and healing can bring significant shifts to clients and asks coaches for focused attention to the client's often subtle and nuanced needs. Engaged with an awareness of both pathogenic and salutogenic approaches, healing-oriented coaching invites both client and coach to hold illness, injury and loss in a healing narrative that makes sense, is manageable and has meaning. Coaches who choose to serve in a healing capacity attune to the shifting dynamics among their clients' current competencies and capacities. They are grounded in the difference between curing and healing—between quantitative and qualitative outcomes—and are present to what is true for their clients while remaining open to what may be possible.

INEVITABLY MESSY

—Reggie Marra

October 1, 2012

My current work with healing explores my parents' and sister's respective dyings and deaths, the violent deaths of several students and classmates, my ongoing struggle to do the work that calls me in a financially sustainable way, and the ripple effects of having both my hips replaced in 2003 at the age of 49.

May 12, 2013

On November 24, 2012, I learned that my just-over-13-year marriage was ending and that my desire to stay, work, and grow together into a deeper relationship will not be fulfilled. Now, the relationship with the woman I deeply loved, and in whose eyes and embrace I'd felt fully seen and loved, continues to dissolve; our house is for sale, our savings are scarce, my current work and income are barely sufficient for basic expenses, and uncertainty about where and how I will live envelops me. In my darkest moments, grief, regret, failure, guilt, anger, shame, doubt, fear, dread, and questions of identity and purpose are my constant companions.

My past engagements with healing have included writing, exercise, meditation, nature, and conversation/relationship. Each of these beckons as I traverse the end of my marriage amid the unfolding of what needs, and will need, to be healed. Beyond the ending itself and what it literally is bringing about, my companions, especially shame, failure, not good enough, and imposter, clamor for attention, and each of them embraces moments of credibility with my most fragile, uncertain self.

I've engaged these five "practices" on a regular, and in some cases, daily, basis for years—not just in times of intentional healing. Each of them calls me to be present and contributes to "perspective-building," especially over time. As I live this marriage's ending, writing—as an exploration of my sense of what is, not as an ongoing litany of complaint—invites and allows multiple perspectives to emerge. Exercise brings a more positive, albeit temporary, and often creative energy, and simply makes me feel better. Meditation allows me to "be with" my pain, my suffering, and how my mind characterizes each amid this ending-in-process. My sitting is difficult and shows me just how unsettled my mind is. Wandering in nature provides a direct and grounding reminder that I can hold my particular "what is" within a much larger and diverse "what is"—and nature never disappoints. Conversation/relationship, for me now the richest and most complex of the five, provides the opportunity for interactive, dynamic perspective-taking and sharing and is my essential practice. Conversation—and silence—with friends with whom I can be raw, open, vulnerable, and real is invaluable. My friends, also, never let me down.

This current, particular grief invites me into an increasingly humble, vulnerable, and connected way of being in all my relationships—family, friends, colleagues, and clients. It's one thing to know that I—we all—suffer and quite another to embody the bio-psycho-social-spiritual symptoms of loss, guilt, fear, shame, anger, uncertainty, and regret. My own healing process allows me to sit with a deeper sense of attunement to the delicate vulnerability of others in my life and to better co-create and hold the safe container of relationship within which we meet. The darker the space I inhabit and work through, the better able I am to be with others in their dark spaces.

When I step back and observe these relationships, be they personal or professional, my healing process also reminds me to hold myself with more compassion and love. Now, when I live an unskillful moment or missed opportunity or feel unsure of a next step, I am sometimes better able to remember that I am, and all of it is, okay—even this, even this. The process is ongoing, inevitably messy, and in its own way "perfect."

At times, as I write, I feel stuck and confused—and at times, increasingly clear. I feel untethered; I have doubt. I trust some things and am uncertain about what I know. I want to be done with it as I move through it. I am deeply grateful to anyone who reads this, for your willingness to be with me as much as these written and read words allow.

August 23, 2015

Thirty-three months have passed since I learned my marriage was ending; thirty-one since my first scribblings here; twenty-four since I moved from our house; and twenty-three since the judge granted the divorce. In the past twelve months I've accepted multiple invitations to do work that integrates my love of writing, poetry, education, coaching, and healing. I have an abiding friendship with my former spouse and a solid relationship with my stepson. I'm in a relationship. My friends are as wonderfully present, goofy, and grave as ever. I laugh often and deeply. Nothing is certain or guaranteed. I continue to heal.

∞

Chapter 2

WORKING WITH HEALING NARRATIVES

WHAT IS A HEALING NARRATIVE?

A Healing Narrative is a story about our healing journey. Everybody
has one, though it often requires a shift from our usual perspective in
order to access it. Discovering and imagining our Healing Narrative
forces us to translate our subjective interpretation of illness, trauma,
or grief into new language. It inspires a focus on integration rather
than disintegration, engaging the inherent power to heal that exists
within all of us. It challenges us to choose a healing path amid all
the possible futures we might imagine.

A client's Healing Narrative documents the journey from the
suffering of illness or loss into a healthier, more coherent new way
of being. Accurate self-observation, assessment, and expression are
essential capabilities for this journey. Writing a Healing Narrative
becomes possible when a client is able to experience enough progress,
either functional or measurable, to express this experience in words. We
can find material for healing narratives in our experience of recovery

from illness, trauma, or grief. We can also look at the whole of a coaching program as the unfolding of the client's Healing Narrative.

SUPPORTING CLIENTS IN WRITING A HEALING NARRATIVE

A Healing Narrative is a self-authored story. There is no best formula. We don't have to be "good" writers. How we tell our story is as varied and unique as how we heal and live our lives. There are numerous opportunities for a coach to engage a Healing Narrative in program and practice design and even in coaching conversations. A Healing Narrative may be built over time within a Coaching Program, developed as an ongoing practice, or offered as a specific one-time assignment that directs the client's attention in a focused manner.

Journaling is a fundamental for Healing Narratives, though not the only approach. Journaling can encourage the client to tune into his or her story, collect objective data, and find expanded or new perspectives incrementally over time. Clients can also use other media—painting, music, digital imagery, etc.—to access and express their narrative, especially if they have expertise or comfort in a particular medium. Writing, however, has been consistently found to provide the most powerful transformative experience. Writing one's own Healing Narrative is a valuable practice. Over time, Healing Narratives evolve and change as life provides new challenges and experiences.

QUESTIONS FOR COACHING CONVERSATIONS

There are many ways "in" to a conversation about healing. Finding the successful access point happens through careful listening by the coach as well as trial and error. One way in may be as simple as a question. A powerful question creates, and often emerges through, the intimacy between coach and client and supports the client in opening to new understandings. The following questions demonstrate a variety of lines of inquiry into healing. They can be useful in coaching conversations or ongoing practice design, and while these questions are effective, the most powerful questions often arise in the moment when coach and client are deeply engaged.

- What would have to be true, in this moment, for you to feel that you are healing / in a healing process?
- When we speak about healing, what does that word mean for you personally? Don't worry about getting it "right." What does it mean *for you*?
- What does this illness give you that you didn't have before?
- What do you check for to determine that you're okay or not okay with what's unfolding?
- What creative drive lies within your illness?
- What comes up for you when you fill in this blank: Healing is _____.
- How is it possible that you could be healing without there being a resolution to your symptoms?
- Do you interpret your situation as good, bad, or neutral? In what ways has this evolved?
- In what ways are your symptoms expressed in body, mind, and spirit? Is there a way to express the growing unity of these in terms of healing?

Ongoing Coaching Practices

- Most of us are very familiar with the suffering and limitations associated with illness, injury, or loss. As a result, suffering often becomes the focal point of our story of dis-ease. But what if we also could look at our challenges as a transformative force, with the ability to open up as much for us as they are closing down? Step into that for a moment. How might you tell the story of your illness from that perspective—seeing it as something with the power to transform and deepen your relationship with yourself, others, and your life?

- What is your personal experience of healing? Or, what is your story of healing? When did your healing journey start? What was happening? Where are you in your journey now? What were the most significant events/milestones in your journey? What/Who helped you in your journey? What were your lessons learned in your journey? If you were to give words of advice to someone amid a healing journey what would they be? What does healing mean to you now?

- When you look back on what you have been going through, what kinds of healing have you experienced? Are there any experiences that stand out as milestones or guideposts on your healing journey?

- In what ways do your symptoms express the deepest truth of who you are now? What new beliefs do you wish to grow in the place of these current beliefs?

- In what ways are you able to tune into your sense of relief in response to the loss of health? In what ways are you able to tune into joy in response to loss of health? (Often lurking beneath illness your body is trying to express something that can't be verbalized – yes, I'm happy I am ill. Now my husband can see what it is like to have to single-handedly take care of house and kids. – Yes, I am relieved to be ill. I finally can get the time off I need to recreate myself … and so on.)

- In what ways are you able to tune in to your grief in response to loss of health? Is this grief connected to a deeper grief? What Path(s) have you taken through the stages of denial, anger, bargaining, depression, and acceptance? Where along the way have you been stuck? In what ways have you completed this journey? How has this process restored your flow of health and aliveness?

- What do you hope for as an outcome or resolution? How much can you allow yourself to connect with both your fears and desires? What is needed in order for each of these to flow freely?

COMING HOME

—Lois MacNaughton

I can't remember a time when I didn't just know that I would be fine. It isn't that anything really significant has ever gone wrong with my health—pretty much the usual stuff: childhood illnesses like the mumps, measles, and chicken pox. No broken bones or anything like that.

I have a perspective on healing—that whatever I have to deal with is an opportunity to grow personally.

Whenever there has been something for myself, or my family, I have researched what is going on to look for the best way to approach the situation.

This doesn't mean that I always find the "answer," but it does lead to finding people who have an understanding and can provide the help, guidance, or whatever is required. It could be a book or a professional that provides what I need. I have never been slow to reach out—even when I went through a period of depression, I sought help so that I could learn what was going on for me and open myself to what I needed to do to address the disconnect I was experiencing and get back to engaging with life.

My experiences have caused me to look more deeply at myself, and through this realize that the healing that happens at the physical level usually has a deeper impact on me emotionally and spiritually.

For me, healing is a significant part of my spiritual journey. I heal in the physical readily but it always feels like something far more profound has healed at a deeper level when I look back on my experiences.

I have never doubted that I would heal and that my physical state would return to at least the state that existed prior to whatever I had to deal with.

I have learned how important others are in relation to my healing process. This happens at various levels—the closest is my family, husband, and sons. When I went through jaw surgery several years ago, my husband and oldest son did Reiki for me right away. As a Reiki Master, I had attuned both of them, and they were prepared to assist my process.

It is important for me to be a partner in whatever healing process I go through—to know what is happening and why and to be actively engaged in the decisions that are made. For my jaw surgery I worked with a large group of professionals. They didn't always agree with each other. I found that a little confusing at first, but as I talked with them and began to grasp the different perspectives related to their roles in the process, I was able to understand how they were working on my behalf and that they wanted the best outcome for me. My relationships with these people were very supportive.

What about the spiritual nature of how I experience healing? Something deep within me believes that I will heal, I will be well. As the date for my surgery drew closer I was sure that fear would arise for me. Fear of the unknown; I had never had surgery before—maybe ignorance is bliss—but there was tremendous unknown in this situation for me. At the time there was a lot of press about people being conscious during their surgery—aware of what the chemicals were doing in their bodies, aware of the pain and frozen in place where they could not express what they were experiencing—awful! This is not what happened for me. The day of my surgery I was calm, felt totally at ease, and knew that I was being supported by my family, the team, and the universe. All went well.

How do I feel about healing? I believe it will happen. I believe it is an opportunity for my personal growth. I look to others for assistance in my healing process in that I gain knowledge and support for my journey. Others do not need to be known in person; there are levels of relationship that range from the impersonal learning gained from a book or on the Internet, to professionals that I have interacted with when I sought their expertise, to those closest to me. All of this brings me home to myself as I gain greater insight into who and how I am in the world.

HEALING NARRATIVE AS A PRACTICE

The need for ongoing practice to build the ability for change in behavior is increasingly accepted in a wide variety of healing modalities and is highly applicable to coaching. At some point in the coaching program the coach may determine that a practice involving the writing of a healing narrative will be beneficial for a client. The following exercise can provide the core for a customized practice that can be engaged for a period of two to three weeks to create a deepening awareness of their relationship with healing.

Reflect upon a time in your life in which you recovered from an illness, trauma, or grief. Take a few minutes to close your eyes and really review the events and experience. Consider the following questions:

- How did I know I was healing?
- What were the signs of my healing?
- What was my experience of healing?
- Was the experience meaningful for me? In what ways?
- How was my healing reflected in others around me?

In a journal, write down the answers to these questions. You may describe the actual event or just the answers; that's your decision.

Do this daily for three days. (The initial reflective meditation can be completed in the coaching session)

On the fourth day, read your journal.

- How do I know that I am healing?
- Are there themes or patterns of my healing experiences?
- In what ways has healing been meaningful for me?
- What meaning(s) do I associate with healing?
- What of these meanings am I seeing in my current situation?

Healing Narrative in a Short Coaching Program

Inquiry into Your Perspective on Healing:

Inquiry is an approach to transformational change that "Action Inquiry" author Bill Torbert states makes us "increasingly capable of listening into the present moment from which the future emerges." The following inquiry practice can be used to develop a Healing Narrative when a structured approach suits the coaching relationship. It can stand alone or be used within a larger program. Between the sessions, the use of chosen actions to deepen the learning adds a great deal of value to this approach.

Coach's introduction to client:

This inquiry is intended to help you explore how your present view of healing is working for you and how you might approach it differently from a new and broader perspective. The intention of this program is to move from an Illness Narrative to a Healing Narrative, a new story about how you approach your own healing, one that resonates with you and supports your ongoing sense of wellbeing.

We will take a preliminary look at the steps during our session today. Then over the next three sessions we will dig more deeply to unpack how you presently feel about your health and how you understand healing. Afterwards you will have the opportunity to write your personal Healing Narrative. The final session will focus on what you have learned and how you want to approach your health and wellness going forward.

THE PROCESS:

Session One:

1. Tell me about what is happening for you now.
   a. What are your thoughts and feelings about this?
   b. What have you been doing about it so far?
   c. What results have you been getting from your actions?
   d. How is the way you are feeling affecting others in your life?

2. If you looked into the future and imagined how your life would be with an increased sense of wellbeing, what would that look like?
   a. Looking at things this way, is there anything you think you could do differently to start creating this new vision of the future for yourself?
   b. How might that improve things for you?
   c. What might you have learned from what has been happening for you?

Session Two:

3. How is your present way of looking at your situation affecting your sense of wellness/illness?
   a. How are the choices you have been making from this perspective working for you?
   b. What thoughts and feelings are you having about how you have been approaching this so far?

4. Considering alternatives … So let's review what you have been doing so far and then consider some alternatives based on the new perspective you have imagined.

   a. This is what I heard you have done in the past. _____. What would you do from the new perspective?

   b. This is how you expressed your feelings about it. _____. How would you feel about the new choice or actions?

   c. This is who you have turned to for support/assistance. _____. Who can you turn to for support/assistance in the imagined future?

   d. This is what you said you have been relying on in the health care system. _____. What can you rely on in the health care system going forward?

   e. This is what I heard you rely on outside the health care system. _____. What can you rely on outside of the health care system going forward?

5. Looking at the two perspectives and the options associated with them,

   a. Which would offer you a greater opportunity for wellness?

   b. What actions might you take from this perspective?

   c. How would that improve your life, your sense of wellbeing?

   d. How would that affect others around you?

6. How does this new way of thinking resonate with you?

Session Three:

7. What is the prevailing need/emotion/value that you are trying to fulfill through how you have been approaching things so far?
   a. What is so important to you about that need/emotion/value?
   b. How does it feel to you?
   c. How has it shown up in your life so far?
   d. How might it show up differently?

8. What actions would you take to manifest your new primary value(s) in the world?

Writing your new story, your Healing Narrative:

Once you have explored the questions in this process fully, put away the answers you have written down. Find a quiet place to sit with what you have uncovered about your perspective on your wellbeing.

1. Let your new story unfold. Then find a journal and write it down.
2. What does it feel like?
3. What does it offer you?
4. How can this new way of approaching things allow you to do what is most important to you in the world?

DEATH AS TEACHER

—Amy Phillips

On May 5th, 2004, my nephew Geoff lost his life. He believed he was going through a portal to "the other side," and I hope he was, but for those who survive him, it looked like crashing into a power plant and creating an explosion that reverberated for miles around. The coroner listed his death as accidental because Geoff's friend told us about his final hours. The ruling was determined by the fact that Geoff didn't really understand that he was going to have to leave his body behind. We, his family and friends, were devastated. A beautiful thirty-year-old being vanished.

I began therapy in earnest that year. I'd just discovered that I was the common denominator in a series of relationships with "unavailable" men, the last experience painful beyond belief. I was also committed to having Geoff's death count somehow, to use the pain of his departure as a quickener that would honour all he'd been to me/us/his tribe, people who were distinctly imperfect but loved him the best way we knew how.

I started the therapeutic use of psychedelics that fall. I was frustrated at not being able to go deeper or access memories from my childhood, and despite a gifted therapist no amount of talk therapy was taking me there. In due course my travels took me to South America to work with the powerful plant teacher Ayahuasca. I decided to take a "very temporary early retirement" to follow what I loved and returned two more times over the course of the next year and a half. My consciousness expanded along with my "fleet" of professional healers.

My goal was to be as healthy as I could be—emotionally, physically, and spiritually—by the time I turned 50. I didn't realize at the time that I had set myself on a trajectory that would, of course, never end. I had a strong intention to "sail through menopause" in contrast to my mother's and sisters' difficult experiences. I also had an inexplicable rash on my face that never quite went away. The homeopath I consulted detected dental toxicity, which homeopathic remedies couldn't penetrate. My dentist of twenty years flatly refused to consider the diagnosis, suggesting instead that I consult a dermatologist. To allay fears of family and friends I followed through with his recommendation and "rosacea"' was deemed the verdict. I didn't buy it. It took two tries before I found a dentist I could trust and who corroborated the diagnosis of deep underlying infection. I proceeded to have significant dental work done (extractions, crowns, bridges) and the rash disappeared within weeks. My system was then able to respond to homeopathic remedies, and I did indeed cruise through menopause, hardly missing a beat.

During my Coaching & Healing research conversations with Joel, it was clear to us both that I had taken an active role in my healing, but he posed a question during our second conversation that gave me pause. Were there any healing moments that were unintentional? At first blush I brought up gardening, which has taken me until now to start loving. Of course, I've heard about the healing nature of nature, but there were always gardeners around and seemingly no need for me. But then a void appeared and I stepped in. My love and appreciation for puttering around outside is growing daily. But it took me some time to get clear on where my healing narrative really started. The catalyst was another death, my mother's, when I was thirty. She was sixty-five and due to be released from hospital in a day, but instead went into cardiac arrest and died on a beautiful summer morning in Vancouver, BC. The pain of her passing blew my heart open. I hardly knew which way was up for the first few days, but when we all congregated in our hometown of Bamfield, the healing began. The ocean helped, as did the familiarity of the terrain and the people I'd known all my life. I began experiencing a depth of feelings I hadn't previously known existed, a massive contrast from the extremely shut down place I'd been in just weeks prior.

Fortunately, the muses (via my sister Nancy) had led me to a healer who had asked questions, listened, and consoled for three straight hours as I wept out the anguish I'd been holding, leaving me open enough to receive the magnitude of what had just transpired. It elicited a whole gamut of emotions, including grief and joy, tears and laughter. I was available like never before.

We held Mom's service in Bamfield and an excruciating pain lodged in my throat the moment we began singing "Onward Christian Soldiers" (I have no idea who chose the music ...). This was later diagnosed as a tonsillitis/strep throat combo. There was still the reception to make it through, and the whole thing was surreal, including serving lemon cake that Mom had made, frozen in preparation for this prearranged "summer holiday." She was everywhere during those first few days, hovering close by and making no bones about it. Travels took funny turns, things disappeared and reappeared, the list went on and on. I stayed in Bamfield for a few extra days to recuperate, sinking gratefully into the bed she always slept in at her brother's, my Uncle Johnny's. My wide-open heart cherished the flannel sheets that hadn't been changed since her visit the previous summer, and I lay there cradled, as it were, one last time.

I returned to my life in the city, deeply grieving but still so full of love. It wasn't until some time afterward that I realized that this openheartedness had been my mother's final gift to me. Although it faded over time, the memory of it has been my guiding light ever since. I know the felt sense of this expansive love, and my life and developmental choices have been guided by this experience. The dynamics in my family were rocky after her earthly presence departed, and there are still some aspects that aren't easy. These show up in other intimate relationships, too, as they are apt to do, but by staying alert and attentive to "what is" I am finding more peace and less suffering. The healing trajectory continues, in me and around me. "I am sorry. Please forgive me. I love you. Thank you."

—Ho'oponopono prayer

Poetry and Healing

Poetry continues to surface as a healing art in an ever-increasing number of conferences, books, articles, and professions across the spectrum of our human experience. Using poetry in coaching is similar to working with a Healing Narrative. As a tool that is common in our coaching programs, it is the very first element in the monthly online meetings that the authors of this book regularly attend. While we may appreciate the poet's craft, and even the worldview through which the poem emerges, each of us engages the poem through our own personal perspectives; we "find ourselves" in an image, metaphor, line, stanza, the music of the language, or the poem as a whole. We embrace our personal, soulful, spiritual resonance with the poem, and in this embrace, we feel, write, and speak our respective ways toward wholeness.

Whether it's Coleman Barks' translation of Rumi,
Boil me some more.
Hit me with the skimming spoon.
I can't do this by myself.

or Naomi Shihab Nye's,
Before you know kindness as the deepest thing inside,
you must know sorrow as the other deepest thing.

We are moved to see our own stories in the poet's gifts.

Try this: find a poem you like (or one you've never read or heard). Read it out loud, perhaps twice. Listen, feel, and look for anything in the poem that resonates with you and use that as a starting point to "talk back" to the poem. What you write need not follow the poem's theme or content, but rather can go in any direction; see where your writing wants to go and follow it there. Don't worry about finishing or getting anything "right"—just write. See what happens. Here's one you can try this with.

New Year's Day, 2005

—Julie Flaherty

Santa Fe snowstorm
Pummeling mountain peaks
Fluffy pillows of snow emerge from the mist
Tantalizing adventurous souls

Red orb plastic sleigh
Rushing riders down white valleys
Small girl gripped between mother's legs
Holding on tight with excitement

Jagged rock formations startle
Rough riders on treacherous terrain
Eerie crackling sounds
Branches snapping
And bones

Healing Narratives and Poetry offer exercises and gateways into healing territory. These access points are essential tools in the coach's tool box. Up next the journey continues with the examination of the overall coaching program utilized by the authors of this book. Certainly not the only way to work with healing in a coaching relationship, the Integral Coaching method offers a comprehensive approach to the process of working with clients as compassionate change agents as well as nourishing healers.

EFFORT AND EASE

—John Stoddart

I express my sorrow through depression. It follows that one aspect of healing for me is to become better able to go through the depths of sorrow rather than package it in the limiting confines of a depressive state. Of course, it's never quite that simple. Sickening and healing are multi-faceted. But it helps to understand this kind of thing. Then one can try a different approach. I love Rollo May's definition of depression: the inability to construct a future. The past has brought me too much sorrow, hence my reticence to create something new. On a physical level it's a little like being choked or paralyzed by fear. I hold my breath in anticipation of the next sorrow. I don't breathe deeply enough to flush my body with fresh oxygen. My blood is too thick to move easily and freely into all my cells. My immune system suffers with the stress of it all.

I was born in paradise. Perhaps, in my shadowy subconscious, I knew it couldn't last. So as a boy I played in the golden light of childhood enough for a lifetime. I was a dramatic little guy who grew up fast and strong and tall and smart. I got sick a lot and injured a lot, and I remember being violently sensitive to cold and to loneliness. A friend nicknamed me Bluffin. Was I really faking the pain I so often felt?

Signs of chronic physical and mental distress began when I was a teenager. At fifteen I experienced a dramatic drop in grades, depression, nausea in gym class, dizziness and loss of balance, and a tendency to lose weight. Each was explainable. I thought, this is just me. A pattern was beginning: signs and symptoms appeared, evolved, either grew or faded, new ones appeared, I adjusted. I did not seek an explanation or help. The connection between the symptoms seemed to be the embodiment of my insecurities, my weakness, an interior world that didn't quite make sense. Unhealed injuries piled up; pain pathways became deep ruts throughout my body. Cognitive challenges began to show. Short-term and working memory diminished. The stress of loss and unexpressed sorrow drove me deeper into depression. Yet, for the first few decades I didn't identify as being sick. I didn't want to be seen as sick, especially mentally ill. Year after year, decade after decade, it would always take an acute, dramatic downturn, a breakdown, accident, injury, loss of a relationship, or job, to focus my attention on the intolerable nature of my predicament. Gradually, I lost the ability to play sports, to work, to look after the day-to-day affairs that keep one's life moving forward. I lost the ability to construct my future. The illness cycle took over as I constantly tried to rise above the forces that seemed to be pulling me down and down and down.

What I'm describing above is my interior experience of an unrecognized, undiagnosed, untreated systemic bacterial infection called Lyme disease, or late stage Lyme in its chronic form. I was 55 when I received the diagnosis. My Lyme doctor and I could easily trace the symptoms back 40 years to the fall of 1967. I was living just over a hundred miles from Lyme, Connecticut, the namesake of the disease and epicenter of its spread in North America. We lived on the edge of a wildlife preserve full of deer. Deer ticks spread the bacteria. It's only after diagnosis and treatment, and only in retrospect that I can see and describe the link between symptoms, the progression, the pattern of not expressing my distress and confusion, and not seeking help for the whole of what I was experiencing rather than getting treatment for just specific symptoms like back pain or depression.

Here's one of my hard-learned tenets for my own healing: first admit when I am not well, accurately assess my situation as best I can, and get help. Then I can start the business of getting better. I often wonder if others experience similar symptoms to me but are able to push them aside. Or perhaps they are able to see them so clearly that they can address them quickly and fully such that the symptoms resolve without ever becoming an illness. Perhaps my state of chronic illness is just my unique way of suffering. What if I had insistently pursued medical support early on? Might I have been successful in interrupting the emerging patterns of chronic illness? Might my life be altogether different?

I can now look back on my childhood and see the roots of how I "welcomed" Lyme disease into my life, why Lyme disease has been necessary for my life journey. It has taken much from me yet it has taught me how to heal, not just the infection itself, but how to heal from my very first childhood losses, those earliest primal sorrows that confronted my sensibility that paradise should be mine forever. I know now that paradise includes sorrow.

Epilogue: It's two years later. I would not write this same healing narrative today. It is still very real and relevant but it is the creation of a moment in time now past. I have more distance from the wounds of illness and the wounds of childhood that contributed to my being open to illness. Every day brings another incremental moment of healing within me. This accumulation has brought me to a new level of wellbeing. I'm physically, mentally, and emotionally stronger and more flexible. Depression is no longer a ruling factor in my life. It is more like a child, holding my hand and looking to me for safety and comfort.

I still experience limiting and evolving symptoms. Another piece of the illness puzzle has come to light: I had a traumatic head injury around the same time as Lyme symptoms began and another one some years before. The emerging science is telling. Concussion can dramatically undermine the integrity of the gut and immune system. Perhaps it was these injuries that left me susceptible to Lyme. I'll never know for sure but the anecdotal details are an important addition to the list of potential triggers for chronic symptoms. And they are helpful in my efforts to create meaning from suffering. Healing for me seems to include this kind of knowledge. But I'm also coming to understand that my disciplined and vigilant collection of information and insight needs to be held lightly. The patterns of illness can be unrelenting. On the flip side, an unrelenting effort to be well can be similarly confining. As I tune in to my new sense of wellbeing, I remind myself to balance effort with ease.

∞

Chapter 3

The Four Stages of the Integral Coaching Journey

To provide a context for how Integral Coaches using the Integral Coaching Canada (ICC) adult development technology approach the coaching conversation, the following section outlines the framework for the overall coaching process. In this section, we will explore in greater depth the four phases of a healing-oriented coaching journey. A client case study will provide illustration at each phase. Our exploration of these four conversations captures a tiny snippet of the Integral Coaching method and is not intended as an overview of or introduction to what the authors experience as a rigorous, challenging, extraordinarily effective and always evolving coaching method. We invite you to see Appendix Two if you're interested in learning more.

Intake Conversation

Our sorrows and wounds are healed only when we touch them with compassion.

—*Buddha*

The initial visit with an ICC Integral Coach is entitled an Intake Conversation. This session is essentially devoted to initiating the connection between the coach and the client. The coach's orientation is one of assessment and acknowledgment. While many formalities of the coaching process do not engage until the second visit, referred to as the Offer conversation, one concrete outcome of the intake conversation is the investigation and articulation of the coaching topic, which will become the focus of the coaching program agreed to by the client and the coach. We will use the terms *coaching topic* and *healing topic* interchangeably.

When a client enters the intake conversation with a coach, the opportunity for deep healing begins. On the surface this conversation may appear to be a getting-to-know-you or please-understand-my-illness interaction. There is, however, much more going on in terms of initiating the coaching relationship and attempting to see the world and the coaching topic through the client's eyes. The opportunity to create a safe space for healing is considerable. The coach's presence is essential in setting the stage for healing work. As the topic for healing is uncovered, the exploration by the coach may reveal new and useful aspects of the client's experience, deepening the understanding of the client's experience and desired outcome.

The intake conversation is composed of two main components:

1. Getting a current picture of what the healing topic looks like today and a view of what lies ahead if the topic is attained.
2. Learning about the client's way of seeing their topic, experiencing and enacting based on what they see, and checking

for how things are progressing; this includes how they make sense of their topic, patterns in perception, and resulting actions.

Integral Coaching relies on gaining a clear understanding of the developmental outcomes of the coaching program in the intake conversation. This healing or *coaching topic* is one that sets the foundation for the rest of the coaching program. Rather than making this initial conversation a fact-finding mission filling in necessary boxes needed to create the program, the coach witnesses the client as a wonderful jewel, dulled by what brings them to coaching and longing for the clarity that realizing their topic may provide. The coach's mission is to gently uncover the many facets of this beautiful gem with curiosity and wonder. This exploration in itself can be healing for the client, given the many different angles of exploration and the client's experience of being seen with unconditional positive regard by the coach.

In refining the coaching topic, the coach asks questions and follows threads of narrative, looking for patterns of meaning and opportunities for healing, which draw the client deeper into his or her own experience. Exploring these patterns offers opportunities to see new perspectives on recurring challenges, creating a deeper and broader understanding of what is happening for the client. The coach's unique expression of presence in the coaching relationship sets a powerful foundation for the client's healing journey. A skillful intake leaves the client with valuable insights and a renewed sense of hope. This can be both healing and empowering for the client.

Case Study: Anxiety about Leaving Her Child
Joel Kreisberg, Coach

Claire is a 34-year-old woman with a 10-month-old child born out of wedlock. She begins her visit by talking about how dissatisfied she is with herself. She was previously divorced several years ago. Now she is living in a seemingly stable relationship with the father of her son. The father travels often, leaving Claire at home most of the week. They live in the San Francisco Bay Area, though all of her friends are back in Arizona, where she previously lived.

The reasons for seeking care are anxiety and fatigue. She would like not to take drugs for her anxiety given that she is still nursing her child. She worries about her son considerably, and checks constantly to make sure he is okay. Claire worked as a massage therapist at a local spa before taking a full-time leave to give birth and care for her son. With her son maturing, she is ready to return to the workplace, but her anxiety is debilitating. She fears leaving her son with anyone other than his dad. She doesn't feel her son is safe, and she keeps an eye on him constantly. This leads to exhaustion, as her mind seems to be full of bad thoughts or imaginings as to what might happen to her son.

I ask about perfectionism and Claire confirms that she indeed likes to make sure everything is fastidiously well tended to: "I'm always thinking that there is someplace better than this." She would like to do more with her life. She makes lists of things to do, feeling she is not really getting anything done.

I ask about her past. Claire is originally from the East Coast of the U.S. and later settled in Arizona. Her dad passed away when she was 15 years old. Though he was an alcoholic, she still felt he loved her. She recalls her mom working all the time and therefore had little time for the children. Claire certainly wants to be a better mom.

She had been with her current partner for seven months when she got pregnant. She feels that he is a good father, but since they don't have much time together, the relationship is strained. He often leaves for the entire work week, returning only for the weekend. At this point, she desperately needs him to attend to their son. She's exhausted and cranky, as is he, so they have little quality time as a couple.

Overall, Claire is concerned for her professional life and feels stuck as a new parent.

We agreed at the end of the intake conversation that her healing topic would be: To be more able to trust that everything will be okay for me and my family without my having to do anything.

Agreeing on a healing topic in this initial visit requires the coach and the client to come to an understanding about the overall goals of the coaching program. This involves active listening, asking powerful questions, and gaining insight into the deep desires of the client. Key to the coaching topic is not only a positive outcome, but one that builds new capacities in a client so that they can move forward without a coach. In this example, the topic not only supports Claire's learning to trust that she and her son will be okay, but it also addresses her tendency to be the one making all the effort. Implicit in this topic is her learning to accept things as they are. Why this is so important to the coaching program will become clearer during the Offer Conversation. Notice that rather than having a goal of less anxiety and more energy—a more typical medical approach to

Claire's anxiety—the coaching topic revolves around doing less and trusting more, and when achieved will support her as other challenges arise in her life. Learning to develop these capabilities would really affect Claire's health. She leaves the initial session hopeful and ready to start.

OFFER CONVERSATION

Curing is what a physician seeks to offer you. Healing comes from within us. It's what we bring to the table. And healing can be described as the physical, emotional, mental, and spiritual process of becoming whole.
—Michael Lerner

Imagine you've been hiking in a beautiful forest. The hike started well. You knew where you were going, and you had enough snacks and water for your intended journey. Somewhere along the way things went terribly wrong. Now you are lost, tired, hungry, and every trick you know to find your way back isn't working. It is deeply important to you to get where you wanted to go.

With head in hands you keep asking yourself, "What can I do?" You look up and a chipper woman (or man) is standing in front of you. She offers you a map, some water, and a snack. More than that, she offers to accompany you along the way, sharing some shortcuts, supporting you as you cut through the heavy brush, and helping you learn some new tricks to make the journey more than you thought it could be.

How would you feel at this point? Most likely you'd feel relieved and heard, just when you thought all was lost. This is a very similar feeling for someone working with a skilled Integral Coach during the offer conversation.

This second conversation literally offers the coaching program to the client. The offer serves as a bridge between how the client is currently approaching their situation and the possibilities for how the client can take a more effective approach to a healing topic. The key elements of an offer conversation include:

- A review of the coaching/healing topic that confirms that the coach has an accurate understanding of both client and topic, including *why* it's important.
- An offer of the client's Current Way of Being (CWOB) in the coaching topic, expressed through metaphor, including how their current approach has supported them so far and how it is interfering with the ability to do things differently going forward. Metaphors are used in ICC's methodology as a way to enable the client to look at themselves through another lens, picture, or prism, without judgment.
- An offer of a New Way of Being (NWOB) in the coaching topic, also a metaphor, including what this new way will support in the client. Integral Coaching works to enable a picture or way of holding a potential future that is within the client's grasp and provides inspiration, hope, and an anchor for new capacity building.
- A proposed coaching program that includes developmental objectives, the capabilities the client will need to develop to support the NWOB in the coaching topic, as well as an initial self-observation exercise to help the client gain a better understanding

of how they are approaching things and a foundation practice to help create better conditions for growth when appropriate.

Metaphors, and perspectives on what they do and how to use them, abound in books and articles across disciplines. Very simply, a metaphor "that works" allows us to see or experience something as or through something else, and if we believe that thing is ourselves, or part of us, an effective metaphor allows us to see whatever it is as an object—out there, and we can more easily befriend and work with it. So the bright, energetic, young, husband, father CFO cancer survivor who wanted his life back was able to work with "The Responsible Librarian" as a way to better see his highly organized, predictable, and knowledgeable current tendencies, and he found value in growing toward the new tendencies that "The Curious Explorer Abroad" suggested might be his. You get the idea.

CASE STUDY CONTINUED:
In the offer conversation Claire was offered the following coaching program:

Her Current Way of Being metaphor is the Conscientious Night-Watchman.

The Conscientious Night-Watchman is focused on protection, in this case with precision and clarity. The night watchman has to keep awake with both eyes open for potential dangers. The Conscientious Night-Watchman really does her job well. Given the circumstances, the challenge is that the Conscientious Night-Watchman doesn't get any time to recharge her battery.

Claire's New Way of Being metaphor is the Trusting Lioness.

The New Way of Being offers a metaphor for Claire to grow into. The Trusting Lioness is not only a strong and powerful image, she is a member of a pride of other mothers that look after their cubs together. The Trusting Lioness is confident that the cubs are safely cared for, not just by her, but by the pride as a whole. As long as she stays connected to the other lionesses, she can count on everything being fine.

The Developmental Objectives are the goals for the coaching program, and they outline the capabilities that are required for success as well as provide a level of measurability to the coaching program overall. Claire will use these developmental objectives to help her build the necessary skills to reach her goals of being more trusting and more comfortable with doing less for her child.

- To be more able to connect to other women who are caring for their children
- To be more able to feel how safe my child is
- To be more able to let others care for me and my child

The coaching program itself required Claire to meet with the coach for several months allowing for a successful transition back to work.

CWOB AND NWOB OFFERS: SHIFT FROM A DISEASE NARRATIVE TO A HEALING NARRATIVE

In working with a healing topic, the CWOB and NWOB metaphors offered by the coach are designed to enable the client to consider a shift from a potential disease narrative—I'm anxious and exhausted—to a healing narrative—I am trusting and more accepting. Honoring the client's CWOB can bring insight into how the current experience of illness might not only be one of suffering, but might also allow for certain valuable experiences. Claire is not asked to "get rid" of her conscientious night watching, rather she is asked to learn that there is a time and a place for this quality that can be beneficial or limiting depending on the circumstances. This requires a delicate inquiry with the client who may find little of value in painful experiences. As a perfectionist, Claire finds it far easier to be self-critical about her overly controlling behavior. The narrative shift offers her the opportunity to find value in her current behavior, while adding a new layer of acceptance and relaxation. The NWOB offers a possibility of a new approach, which if practiced by the client, can fulfill her inherent yearning for a healthier way of living.

In the context of a coaching topic, the intentions of the CWOB and NWOB offers are presented in the following graphic.

CWOB	NWOB
• Disease Narrative • Ways of seeing, going, and checking that reinforce a limiting state • Resistance to the way things really are • Probabilities thinking • Makes best effort to adapt to personal suffering using current competencies • Finds comfort, familiarity and value in CWOB's strategy • Letting go	• Healing Narrative • New ways of seeing, going, and checking that nurture healing • Increasing acceptance of the way things really are • Possibilities thinking • Cultivates new 'healing Pathways' through competency development • Transcends and includes the CWOB • Letting come

Cycles of Development

Healing always comes from within, even when sparked and evoked by someone or something outside ourselves. We are each our own healer and that deeper well of love is our ultimate healing force.

—John Stoddart

Human beings grow and develop incrementally. Cycles of Development, the ongoing sessions in a coaching program, direct the client's unique developmental objectives into essential capabilities, small steps that can be successfully realized and embodied by the client. Each cycle of development conversation allows the coach and client to return to the client's topic, check for subtle or significant shifts, then explore and calibrate the next capability to work on.

The goal of each cycle of development is to provide supportive self-awareness and dynamic coaching interactions. In between cycles of development sessions clients develop their skills by working with a focus practice, offering the client a new "doing," a way to approach and practice this "doing" in their day-to-day life, and reflection questions to deepen and anchor new understanding. Assigned practices may also include foundation practices, ongoing exercises that build a supporting capability needed for the client to be successful in his or her topic. Both focus and foundation practices are custom-designed to support the incremental steps needed for the client to further embody each new capability necessary for each developmental objective. The coach points out the client's New Way capacities showing up, identifying shifts from, and inevitable resistance-based returns to, their Current Way, which is ultimately transcended and included in their New Way.

Transforming Disease Patterns into Healing Patterns

Coaches are alert to patterns. Both illness and healing are constellations of patterns and each cycle of development is an opportunity to reveal, interrupt, and shift patterns of behavior that support illness, and to develop and nurture those that enhance healing. In the intake session, clients are assessed for levels of competency in several human development lenses to explore how they experience illness (See Appendices 1 and 2 for a full explanation of Ken Wilber's AQAL system and Integral Coaching Canada's basic framework). By looking closely at the individual's expression of symptoms through multiple perspectives of the AQAL system, deeper and more nuanced opportunities for healing become available.

For example, let's consider clients who experience chronic pain, which is an energy pattern that affects the body, mind, and spirit. Clients interpret pain through conditioned thoughts and emotional responses. The natural response is to pull away. Many try to separate themselves from the pain in an effort to experience relief. In a chronic situation this goes on endlessly in the background, and though pain may appear to be managed, it can leave clients exhausted and debilitated. Pain often shapes the client's views of self and the world. A developmental goal can be to reinterpret the physical or emotional responses to patterns of pain. By using focus and foundation practices, the coach introduces techniques for bringing different attention to pain sensations, offering clients the opportunity to observe subtle shifts in pain sensations throughout the body. These shifts can open up new links to external and internal influencing factors. The client has the opportunity to experiment with the new technique or "doing" and can assess the value and efficacy for themselves. As well, new ways of interpreting these sensations may become available. Over time this process of observation and reinterpretation informs the healing patterns, expanding clients' relationships with pain.

Clients may have thoughts, beliefs, and coping skills that have a natural resistance to change, reinforcing chronic illness patterns. Ongoing coaching sessions offer the potential for the client to develop new ways of understanding aspects of their current habits embedded in chronic patterns of illness. While painful, these patterns often serve some purpose that can be uncovered offering further opportunity for healing to occur.

Building Ongoing Self Observation Skills

Self-observation is necessary throughout this phase of the coaching program, providing a carefully targeted opportunity for clients to see and feel their attachment to their Current Way identity and grasp the depths of suffering that this attachment creates. Often, this helps engage a desire to move beyond the old patterns, which can jumpstart the ongoing, objective, incremental process of the client's dis-identifying with symptoms as they shift from a disease narrative to a healing narrative. Self-observation exercises provide a valuable opportunity for grounding and nuancing skill development that can then be expanded throughout the whole of the coaching program.

In a healing context, building ongoing self-observation skills, along with the objective collection of data, is essential for two key reasons. First, it counters the intensely subjective influence of, and tendency to fixate on, illness symptoms and the embodiment of these patterns. Secondly, it provides essential information for one's circle of support—caregivers and medical and healing practitioners—such that treatment and other healing supports can be more accurately and effectively focused.

It follows that learning to skillfully communicate both subjective and objective experiences may be fundamental to developing healthier relationships at a time when one may be experiencing a sense of loss of self, an increased dependence on others, and isolation from normal everyday activities that most people take for granted. Such circumstances tend to reveal the limitations of cultural and societal systems' abilities to offer adequate support that respects individual dignity. When sick, clients may find it necessary to fight for basic rights at a time when their function and abilities are compromised.

Shifting from a disease narrative to a healing narrative requires that clients counter the tendency to contract and collapse in the face of illness symptoms. The expansive exercise of "this and" is a good example of how coach and client can explore the "more" side within multiple aspects of a client's perspectives:

"I feel depressed *and* I can actually feel gratitude;"

"I feel tired, my legs are still weak, *and* yet I was able to walk for three more minutes today;"

"My wife still thinks I need to just get over myself, *and* I was able to hear her and respond neutrally with some objective information."

We are not advocating a "get positive" approach, but instead an approach that takes in more perspectives, difficult ones and easy ones, while building a wider set of capacities and ways of engaging in healthy and supportive ways of being with illness.

Calibrating Scope and Scale

Though we are often attracted to quick fixes and cures, coaching requires an incremental, steady, and patient approach. As with other forms of change, healing is rarely instantaneous. Small, continuous steps reveal the essential and gradual nature of the healing process.

Coaches must always keep in mind that clients are unique, talented, and creative individuals, and we must attune to the subtle and mysterious nature of each individual's transformation. Healing is supported when we provide an appropriately scaled suite of practices that employ and build on each new capacity within the identified developmental objectives, while taking full advantage of a client's stronger capabilities in order to effect change.

The consequences of illness ripple through all aspects of our lives, affecting relationships, jobs, energy, finances, and motivation, to name a few. Envision a client with 20 years of chronic pain, wanting to find a greater sense of purpose in her life. She describes how her condition strains the relationship with her husband, how she doesn't know when she wakes up whether she'll have the energy to face her day, and how she is still grieving the loss of her father which occurred over a year ago. She is no longer able to read a book because of difficulty in focusing her energy on this type of task. As we design a coaching program for this client, we recognize the importance of pacing and proper scale in designing developmental objectives and coaching practices. Goals must be meaningful for our clients, yet success in building capacity in a New Way of Being is more attainable if the exercise is at the proper scale. This calls for refraining from overly ambitious goals on the part of the coach. Creating practices small enough to be successful, even on our client's worst day, is a necessary skill in working with illness in a coaching setting.

A client (or a coach) may anticipate that a coaching program might provide the same type of relief as one would seek through a medical protocol. As coaches, we must observe such expectations closely, as the coaching program may not be long enough to create the kind of change for which a client hopes. This reinforces the importance of a realistic and effective iteration of the coaching topic, and also points forward, reminding the coach to keep a close eye on wording and achievability of developmental objectives as the ongoing coaching sessions unfold. Adjustment of scope and scale may be required. This kind of adjustment is often experienced during symptom flare-ups, either due to the progression of illness or as a client tries new approaches and therapies, which sometimes work, sometimes don't, and sometimes plateau.

As coaches working in a healing context, we can learn a great deal from our clients, and we practice being alert to the need for checking in on our mutual expectations. This type of checking can be healing as it promotes a fresh perspective of progress and expectations. It's helpful to look at healing as a change of state, something that both coach and client can cultivate more and more deeply over time. A coaching program may simply establish the opportunity for a client to experience a felt sense of their healing, in contrast to a long-felt state of disintegration into illness. Even a glimpse of what it's like to integrate healing can create a powerful opportunity for transformation that may sustain a client well beyond the completion of the coaching program.

CASE STUDY CONTINUED:

Over the course of six sessions, Claire was given two types of practices: focus practices, which focused on the specific developmental objectives, and foundation practices, which offered her regular practice for growing into her NWOB. The initial self-observation exercise brought awareness to Claire of the way the Conscientious Night-Watchman attends to details and how this attention affects Claire's sense of connection to her son, her boyfriend, and herself. Her foundation practice asked her to find a local teenager to hire to spend time with her and her son in the home. The goal of this latter assignment was not to leave her son with the new care person, but rather to get used to having someone else being around her son and perhaps to create some personal time for Claire.

For each coaching cycle, Claire was given a focus practice cultivating the new way of being, the Trusting Lioness. In the first of these, Claire invited a neighbor's daughter in to care for her child. She noticed how her anxiety kept her clinging to her thoughts and truly exhausted her. Having another person definitely helped with her anxiety, but she was just beginning to see how much her anxiety was crippling her. Her next focus practice asked Claire to choose one person each day, someone that she might already be spending time with, and pay attention to connecting to that person with her heart, appreciating what is special about him or her. The foundation practice changed from having the teenager in the home, to finding another mom with a child and arranging play dates for both her and her son together. The reason for this was that I felt that Claire needed someone she could better relate to—so this assignment was about finding a "pride" to belong to.

These practices went very well. Claire made a decision to join a Baby Boot Camp group with other mothers and young children. She made more connections there with peers, finding it easier to relate to other moms. She had far less time alone with her anxiety. She reported, "I've become aware that at times when I was so closely paying attention to my son, I felt that I didn't deserve to be treated any better. Now I feel more comfortable with him while with others. I feel better about myself now, too."

Her third focus practice asked her to notice several times a day when she has the desire to step in and protect her son, to pause, take a breath and say to herself, "Everything is following its natural flow," followed by a surrender to what is happening. From there she could do whatever naturally came next. This wasn't asking her to change her behavior, rather, just to pause and remind herself that what is happening is natural. As she did this she was to notice whether and how the Conscientious Night-Watchman or the Trusting Lioness might show up. The foundation practice continued to be to spend at least one session a week with another mom with a child. A third foundation practice was offered—practicing basic mindfulness for five minutes daily. Claire was given meditation instructions.

The next visit occurred immediately after Claire had returned to work for two days. She had found a day-care setting that worked for her and her son. She was able to let her son be without her for those two days. While a bit sad and worried, Claire was pleased she had made it back to work, planning on working two days each week. She said, "Every once in a while I get anxious, but it tends to go away." Rather than being torn about the challenges of being a working mother, she was noticing that her relationship with her partner was becoming first and foremost in her anxiety. This is not uncommon in a coaching program, in that as new awareness skills grow, different issues surface that may have been buried underneath old patterns. The new focus practice asked Claire to pay more attention to her own needs for intimacy—she was to ask her boyfriend to make time for her in his life and for the two of them to have a date night. The attention was on how to reconnect to her relationship (rather than their child or to other mothers) and to notice how this would affect Claire. The foundation practices didn't change.

COMPLETION CONVERSATION

A Completion Conversation accomplishes many things in addition to wrapping up a coaching program. The path forward is mapped out by grounding clients in a deeply embodied understanding of where they have come from and where they have arrived, always defining their growth in relation to their topic. Wholehearted appreciation is central to this process. A deep sense of honor and compassion is brought to bear on aspects of the client's Current Way of Being that are irrefutably essential to who they are as a person. Developmental objectives are reviewed and gains made throughout the time together acknowledged and celebrated. The conversation naturally turns to the ongoing journey that still lies ahead and the lifelong capacities that will help the client along their way. Suggestions are made for supportive resources moving forward as they prepare to take the next steps on their own.

As with any topic, the coach and the client decide together when it is time to bring the program to an end. This precept is a good way to remind ourselves as coaches that healing is ultimately in the mind, body, and spirit of the client.

Completing well is fundamental to a powerful coaching program. How does a coach approach completion when healing is a consideration? Here are a few things to keep in mind as your client is ready to complete their coaching sessions:

- Coaching should support healing from start to finish
- Healing is spontaneous, ongoing, and often incremental
- Healing continues at one's developmental edge

In Integral Coaching, the coach unflinchingly supports the client's incremental shift from their Current Way disease narrative to their New Way healing narrative. The completion of the coaching program happens in relationship to the client's healing experience, rather than being directly tied to the client's healing outcomes. In completion, the coach must continue to steadfastly walk the territory of illness and healing with the client, alert to the natural and ever-present tendency (of coach and client) to measure outcomes in terms of improvement of symptoms.

Any change in symptoms can illustrate and support the embodiment of the client's shift from a Current Way to their New Way. In this sense, a client might experience an increase in severity of symptoms and still experience healing in their core experience of the illness. For example, a client might experience an increase in physical pain, yet develop greater integration with their way of understanding and relating to that pain, improving their ability to accurately communicate and share their experience with others.

Case Study continued:

The coaching program was coming to a close. Having successfully returned to the workplace for two days a week, Claire was quite pleased: "I love it. I have time for myself." She was doing better with her partner, which was also helping him. This doesn't mean everything was perfect. Claire was still worried about her relationship because of the demands that her partner's work continued to place on him. Yet Claire's overall health had improved—her energy was better and her anxiety about her son was now minimal. She slept better, though sometimes work issues did keep her up at night. Making career moves was moving front and center. Claire had created several stable relationships with other moms. She was more trusting that her son was in good hands with others, and she was better able to attend to a strained relationship with her partner. In the present, the coaching topic, trusting that everything will be okay for Claire and her family without having to do anything, has been achieved.

It is clear then that healing is not synonymous with curing, and that Integral Coaching in a healing context includes both perspective-shifts and increased self-awareness as well as the related changes in experience and behavior. The circumstances may not have changed but how the client understands and responds to them has grown. Through these four phases of the Integral Coaching process the client has the opportunity to meet his or her illness or pain in a new way, a way that allows for and facilitates changing the relationship with these aspects of self. Through these changes of understanding healing can occur. The guiding role of the coach is twofold, keeper of coaching form and structure and torch bearer, leading the way into new opportunities and awareness.

Climbing Back in the Sangre de Christos
—Julie Flaherty

I remember the accident clearly—the round, red sled my young daughter and I were riding on launching into what appeared to be giant pillows of fluffy snow. Unfortunately, under the soft snow were jagged rocks, which our sled descended upon. My young daughter was unscathed, but I heard my bones cracking upon impact and was struck with dizzying pain by the time our sled reached the bottom of the hill. X-rays revealed a severely broken back. Serendipitously, we had been visiting my brother in Santa Fe, who was the only other person I knew who had recovered from a broken back. I'd coached him through meditations for pain control and had taught him energy work when he had been "flat on his back" years before. He recalled what had worked best for him and we created a similar healing regime of prayer, meditation for pain control, and energy work.

Lying flat in bed in a body cast for months following the accident, with pain so intense it felt like lightning bolts shooting through my pelvis and back, provided tremendous motivation to focus on healing. I prayed and meditated for many hours each day. The pain moderated as mental clarity gradually returned. With the help of a skilled paraplegic yoga instructor, who had learned yoga after he lost the use of his legs, I regained the ability to stand and walk. I began to live my understanding of the mind-body connection, learning to see pain as a flow of energy (albeit an acutely intense flow!) instead of an unwanted force that I tried to squirm away from. My deepening mind-body connection, as well as a rejuvenated faith and spiritual connection, were powerful resources.

A few years later, another opportunity for healing ripened. I learned that my mother had been prescribed the drug DES to reduce the chances of miscarriage during her pregnancy. We now know that DES causes birth defects, including the congenital hip dysplasia which I was born with. A strong yoga practice had delayed surgery for decades, but finally total hip replacements of both of my legs were unavoidable. Due to a number of medical mishaps, including a surgeon accidentally breaking my femur during hip surgery, I have had six surgeries over the last three years. Having progressed from a wheelchair, to crutches, to two canes, and now one, my intention is to be able to walk unassisted one day.

During this time I've been sustained by an incredible community of family, friends, other parents from our small school, and my faith community. After each surgery this amazing community—who knew me as a single parent with my children full time—would fill in the gaps for me, bringing meals, books, medical supplies, offering companionship and deep spiritual connection. This groundswell of nurturance was one of the most powerful resources for our family's healing, allowing my daughters and me to survive each day, knowing we were loved and cared for.

For the first few surgeries, I wholeheartedly believed the surgeon's opinions as to how long recovery would take, and felt angry, sad, frustrated, and discouraged when the results were worse than their predictions. As I prepared for the latest surgery last month, I realized my attitude had shifted from expecting my body to meet a typical timetable and instead to "let what will be, be." This is a huge shift from my earlier attitude of expecting and desiring certain outcomes. When I think this way, I feel more relaxed and am less hard on myself. This time, I am open to the best outcome, but I am also making back-up plans in case it does not happen. I might have thought of this as negative thinking previously and chastised myself for it, but now it feels like self-care. There is a sense of curiosity and playfulness I feel as I wait for the "mystery" to emerge. I feel safer in the world.

Peter Levine's "In an Unspoken Voice" speaks potently to my own experience of healing: "Trauma sufferers, in their healing journeys, learn to dissolve their rigid defenses. In this surrender they move from frozen fixity to gently thawing and, finally, free flow. They come to know their bodies and know embodied life, as if for the first time. While trauma is hell on earth, its resolution may be a gift from the gods."

∞

Chapter 4

CASE STUDIES

Healing is a lifelong journey in which each individual's path is unique. It is an integrative process that encompasses the entire spectrum of our existence—physical, mental, emotional, spiritual. The healing process helps us to find meaning by asking what is right with ourselves and exploring our most fulfilling ways of being, relating, and creating the world. It makes our perspectives wider and broader.

—Smith Center for Healing and the Arts

Healing occurs in many forms, and coaching varies considerably from coach to coach, even among coaches who share a common method. This section presents five case studies that demonstrate some of the principles discussed earlier in this book. The cases are not offered here to limit or define how coaching in a healing context should emerge, but rather to offer the reader an opportunity to more closely engage examples of how theory, principle, and method actually manifested in practice.

Each of these case studies offers its own unique snapshot of healing and coaching. The first, "A New Way of Being: Metaphor as a Pathway to Self-Healing," follows Alex's work with Olivia, a mother of four who's living into her diagnosis of multiple sclerosis. As Olivia works with her chronic condition, the metaphor, "Dorothy and her Friends from the Wizard of Oz," serves her in her healing journey, both during the coaching and long after the coaching program has ended.

In the second case study, "Appreciating What Is More Than What Should Be," Jason is struggling with chronic fatigue. Through working with his coach, Lois, he comes to recognize just how much his current way of being in the world was deepening his fatigue. Through this increased self-awareness, he is able to relax and begin to find a new way that allows him to be with what is, rather than drive toward what should be. His symptoms of fatigue provide an important message that demands his attention and then serves him well.

Case study three, "Using the Healing Narrative as a Focus Practice," offers a glimpse into the specific use of a healing narrative within a coaching relationship. As a means of framing profound shifts in the coaching program, Alex asks Martin to work with his healing narrative. The narrative process reveals key insights that help focus the healing work. Revisiting the healing narrative at the close of the coaching program provides the client with a powerful opportunity to look back at and take a fresh perspective on his earlier point of view, which facilitates even deeper healing.

In "Step by Step by Step," case study four, John coaches Rick, who is living with a condition called achalasia. Because Rick is a competitive athlete, the condition challenges the very core of his understanding of who he is. Through the power of metaphor and a healing narrative, Rick is able to significantly change his relationship not only with his body, but with his sense of identity, allowing him to understand his condition and himself with greater acceptance and curiosity. Rather than something to be cured and discarded, achalasia becomes for Rick an opportunity to explore a wider, deeper version of his life.

Finally, "Liberating Paralyzing Internal Blocks," offers a detailed view of the full coaching process in action. In this fifth case study, the coaching and healing conversation focuses not on illness, trauma, or loss, but on the client's overcoming a profound perceptual and behavioral limitation. Here, Amy coaches Alex, who is unable to submit any of the six novels she has written for publication. Her anxiety about revealing herself to others seems to counter her desire to express herself through her written work. The coaching process, which is significantly healing for her, allows her to accept herself and show up more fully as a writer, mother, spouse, and daughter.

CASE STUDY ONE: A NEW WAY OF BEING: METAPHOR AS A PATHWAY TO SELF-HEALING
Alex Douds, Coach

When we started coaching in 2010, Olivia was 38 years old, the mother of four children, and working as a freelance writer. During a trip to Spain in 2007 she had a stroke that was diagnosed as multiple sclerosis (MS). Life became much more challenging with the MS as she had to find ways to conserve energy, reduce stress, and still fulfill her perceived responsibilities as wife, mother, writer, etc.

Since Olivia was experiencing severe writer's block particularly around writing things in her own voice, we agreed that her topic was that she wanted to find and trust her voice as a writer. As she expressed it, this involved being able to honor her own subjectivity over objective standards, allowing for vulnerability, and resisting the urge to seek permission from others. This topic was important because Olivia had a deep desire to leave a lasting record of herself through her writing.

Olivia's CWOB metaphor was Living in a Safehouse. In order to keep her inner world safe and identity protected, she needed to keep the appearance of being perfect and meeting the external expectations of others. This CWOB metaphor enabled her to look at herself from another vantage point including how this current way supported her in some ways but also interfered with her ability to express and trust her own voice.

Her NWOB metaphor was Dorothy and her Friends from the Wizard of Oz. This NWOB metaphor enabled Olivia to picture a potential future that was within her grasp and would serve as an anchor for building new capacity. In order to find and express her own voice, Olivia, like Dorothy, learns to use the qualities of her three friends: the courage of the Lion (a voice that is powerful and strong—it can roar when it needs to); the heart of the Tinman (a voice that speaks from the heart); and the brains of the Scarecrow (a voice that is clear and effective); as she travels on the yellow brick road to reach her destination and find her way home (expressing her voice).

Her developmental objectives addressed expressing her voice in difficult situations, engaging in the lighter side of life with others, being kinder to herself, and being more connected to and honoring what deeply matters. By the completion of coaching, Olivia had made much progress in her coaching program; she not only was writing a memoir, but also created her own blog related to MS. Some of her progress was reflected in a touching email just prior to our completion conversation:

Hi Alex,

Wanted to share an exciting update, something huge and pretty personal. You really touched a nerve when you talked about how I lost my childhood when we moved to California when I was 13. It's true that I became very serious and careful after that, except for one summer during my teenage years when I had a boyfriend and we had so much fun going to the lake, swimming, driving around, and laughing endlessly. It struck me that I needed to know more about the girl in that window of time. I hadn't thought about anything to do with that period in years, and my memory was pretty fuzzy. So I meditated and built up a well of courage and called this man, to whom I have not spoken in twenty years. I was totally honest and explained why I was calling, told him all about my MS and my coaching. He was a little taken aback, given it was the middle of his workday. But he kindly took the time to share his memories with me about what was fun then, what sort of person I was, and how he remembers that girl and all the silly jokes we used to tell each other, some of which were still funny. I found the whole experience hugely healing to be able to talk to someone who knew the carefree Olivia.

One thing he said to me that really touched me and brought tears to my eyes was, "Olivia, if there is anyone who can handle something like MS, it's you." I felt this was such a vote of confidence because this person really knew me before I became so overly careful and afraid of everything.

I just wanted to share that with you and tell you thank you so so much for helping me to learn to soften up enough to ask the questions and take the actions I need to take in order to be well.

At our completion conversation, Olivia expressed a desire to periodically check in, so I've continued to see her about three times a year, interspersed with periodic emails. During our check-ins (I don't think of these as coaching conversations) it has become evident that the way of Dorothy and her Friends and her ever-growing capabilities have not only been sustained but continue to develop in how she relates to herself and others. Olivia reports dramatically different relationships with her husband to whom she is able to speak with a more authentic voice; her children to whom she is able to relate as individuals and respond to their unique needs; her parents with whom she has been able to break long-lasting patterns that kept her in a subservient role; her doctors whom she is able to question and challenge when needed; and her bosses and colleagues at work with whom she is unafraid to share a different perspective and disagree. As her progress continues she frequently makes reference to how she has drawn on the optimistic, open-hearted spirit of Dorothy, the humor and courage of the Lion, the bark of Toto, the open-heartedness of the Tinman, and the smarts of the Scarecrow.

During the past year, I received an email from Olivia. Usually, I initiate the check-in emails to Olivia, so this was a first. Part of the email mentioned some recent medical feedback:

On a brighter side, my brain scan results came back and the news was great. The nurse said that the radiologist had written in the report "no sign of MS." How's that for something to get excited about.

My response:

I'm so excited to hear about your news from the radiologist but also curious. What does it mean when you say no sign of MS? Is it possible for MS to go into remission? On a couple of occasions when we last talked you mentioned that the symptoms of MS have subsided in your life. As you know I have an interest in learning more about the process of healing. I'd love to learn more, if you're willing to share.

Olivia's response:

I am feeling fine. You asked about my MS. What it all means is that I had a clear brain scan. I keep wondering if I have been cured or if it was a false diagnosis in the first place, etc. Honestly I don't know. About 5 percent of patients have a clear brain scan. I don't know how to frame it and that is difficult for me. My neurologist is a kind and sweet man. I spoke to him about this confusion, and he observed that I am the kind of person who likes to understand things, but unfortunately that is not possible right now. Something about that compassionate acknowledgment really touched me. It brought tears to my eyes. So for now, I am just trying to stay grateful for my good health and not wonder too much what the future might hold. No one knows, right?"

My response:

I'm so appreciative you're willing to share with me about your MS experience. I loved the response of your neurologist to your inquiry when he acknowledged your need for understanding and that he unfortunately couldn't provide any answers; it's a mystery. What a lovely interaction. It's so human to say "I don't know" even when society expects physicians to have the answers. I also deeply appreciate and respect your response to your mystery, to accept that no one really knows, and to be grateful for each day, each moment, each conversation with your children where you learn a little more about what they are becoming—about their mystery. Again thanks for sharing. I hope we can continue to talk about your journey toward wellness and wellbeing.

Olivia's response:

Your email was so thoughtful. It really made me think. (As always!) It hadn't occurred to me that the doctor could have blustered some response. Yes, I am fortunate to have such an honest and kind doctor. As for the MS, sometimes I feel a little panic when people (kind-hearted no doubt) imply that it was all a big mistake and that perhaps I have something else. Such statements awaken a deep sense of dread that I might have to undergo another process of medical discovery. Because it's all so tender and I'm just finding my way, I have chosen not to share it with people outside of my trusted circle. Sometimes I get the feeling that people want to "close the book" on things they don't understand. After a death, after a crisis, after whatever, they want it to be all over, wrapped up, problem solved. That's just not possible with this situation, although, yes, the crisis appears to be over and indeed, for now, the problem is solved.

In our work as coaches, we frequently don't know about the lasting power of the NWOB metaphor and the capacities that continue to emerge beyond the completion conversation. My sense is that the meaningfulness of the NWOB will vary from client to client. Clearly, as in Olivia's case, some clients are stimulated to continue a deeper and perhaps more sustainable healing narrative. I think that her NWOB thoughts, feelings, and capabilities have been and continue to be a magical self-healing journey that has no end in sight, just a lot of new beginnings. Life truly is an unfolding mystery if we are open to it.

CASE STUDY TWO: APPRECIATING WHAT IS MORE THAN WHAT SHOULD BE
Lois MacNaughton, Coach

Jason came into coaching after being diagnosed with chronic fatigue. Since the diagnosis he had tried a variety of traditional and non-traditional measures to address his situation and was feeling disgruntled at the lack of improvement he was seeing relative to his efforts. His way of approaching everything was to take it on himself, work until he was exhausted, and then crash. Crashing was the only way he could allow himself to take a break, and even then he felt guilty. This approach was not going to allow him any ease from the chronic fatigue or allow the enjoyment and fulfillment he desires in life.

During the offer conversation the coaching relationship truly found its ground as I presented the metaphors for his current and new ways of being. The image of his current way, the Exhausted One-Man Band resonated and it was clear that Jason felt he had been heard at a deep level. On presenting the Receiving Ever-Renewing Forest tears welled up in his eyes and he asked, "How are we going to do it?" Hope was alive and he knew he couldn't do it alone, which was already a new move for someone with a solitary approach.

The coaching relationship is an entity in and of itself; it contains both coach and client in a safe and trusting space. Neither of us was the leader or the follower; it became a dance, each of us responding and not trying to control the outcomes, just allowing co-creation to emerge. This didn't happen automatically. As the coach I already trusted the process, but it took time for him to surrender to it. After several cycles of development he was feeling confused but committed.

"I don't know how this is supposed to work, but I'm not going to give up."

Getting fully acquainted with the Exhausted One-Man Band was draining and frustrating for both of us at times. As coach, I knew that true compassion was critical. When he resisted what was arising emotionally, he was in significant discomfort. Without the support of the relationship he could easily have slipped away from the new awareness and back into his old pattern. The practices I created for him needed to be scaled to fit into his already over-full schedule so that they wouldn't add to the burden, and they would create awareness and the potential for change at the same time. Coming into a session he frequently said, "I don't think this is what you were expecting." As a perfectionist (Enneagram type 1) personality who is action-oriented, he came to the realization that he didn't have to live up to expectations only through the constant reminder that there were no specific expectations, only a hope that awareness and the potential for what works for him would emerge. This allowed for simpler, smaller things to begin having impact on how Jason was seeing and responding to his world. He saw our coaching relationship as a place to redefine self-imposed boundaries and to explore different dimensions and different ways of experiencing.

During the fifth cycle of development conversation the full impact of his current way became very clear, and I could see the energy dropping in him as it happened. He saw that all of the pressure he puts on himself had been exacerbating, and may even have contributed to, his chronic fatigue. He was letting go and it was uncomfortable but we sat with it together. As we sat, his energy began to shift, and it was like watching a light come on as he recognized that what had seemed to require so much effort didn't actually. He became lighter and started to see how the chronic fatigue had allowed him to stop, something that had not been an option in the past. In his own words, "And then it came together all on its own—it self-integrated. I couldn't think my way through it; the way it came together was an experiential moment, but all of a sudden it all made sense."

Within the coaching relationship he has come to appreciate *what is* more than *what should be*. Finding out what the chronic fatigue brings to his life has allowed the appreciation of what is available rather than what is idealized. Jason has opened up to the idea he can receive and stop, that it would now be possible to pause, to rest, and just enjoy being. It was time to start letting come.

Case Study 3: Using the Healing Narrative as a Focus Practice
Alex Douds, Coach

Martin, a teacher in a private school in Germany, found himself in a pattern of returning from work very tired, distracted, and unable to engage in pursuits that truly mattered to him. In his words, he was numbing out on life and was deeply concerned. Since he had successfully worked with a coach in the past, he decided to seek out coaching services again.

Coaching topic: I want to increase my capacity to accept, love, and care for myself and enjoy life each day as I continue my interesting life journey.

Current Way of Being: the way of the Demanding Artist Striving for Perfection.

New Way of Being: the way of Buddha's Heart

Developmental objectives:

- I am increasingly able to discern on a daily basis when I have done enough in my striving and when I deserve to take time for me, whenever that might be.
- I am increasingly aware of what's happening in my mind and body in the present moment without trying to control, judge, or pull away.
- I am increasingly able to be compassionate, kind, and loving toward myself.
- I am increasingly able to receive gratitude, acknowledgment, and appreciation from others as heartfelt forms of caring and affection for me.

Context for developing a Healing Narrative as a Focus Practice:

About mid-way through the coaching program it appeared that a profound shift was occurring in the client's way of being. To capture the story and meaning of this shift I asked the client to complete the following practice:

Focus Practice: Reflecting on Your Coaching Journey Through Story:

Before we meet next I'd like you to create a narrative—a story—of your coaching journey thus far by describing where you started and this beautiful shift in perspective that has started to emerge for you. Below you will find some questions that will help you create your narrative. Please feel free to generate your own questions that help to capture your journey as a personal story. Initially, just record your thoughts to these questions in your journal. At some point you will feel ready to build your story from your responses to the questions.

Go back in time and connect with the person you were in our first meeting.
- What words would you use to describe him? What was his way of feeling, thinking, and acting in the world? What results was he getting?
- What words would you use to describe the person you are today? What has shifted for you? What are examples of this shift?
- What do you think most significantly contributed to these changes in you?

Martin's Healing Narrative

At the start of the coaching program, I was a person who wanted to feel at ease with himself, comfortable, and open to challenges. However, I had a real fear that that was not actually possible because I hadn't found a way yet. My way of dealing with that upset was to detach from my body, stay in my mind, and be occupied with a frequent feeling of not deserving to be loved. I held a sense of lack, of ongoing pressure, taunting, disapproval, and internal bullying that would always be in the background. It was so common to me, that it was basically a given. I didn't like it, but felt as though the only way out was to find ways to let it be there and also try and be happy at the same time, despite an underlying current of self-contempt.

I saw the world as a place where it was wrong to exist. For all of the joy, happiness, and fun I could have with myself or others, ultimately just being alive brought with it a shame and a sense of being undeserving of being at ease in this life.

The result was that I couldn't find the ease I wanted in life. Whenever I turned towards what I enjoyed, I felt I wasn't deserving of the happiness I was getting. When I felt like trying to argue against my internal critics, I found that they always had a trump card and won out with something like, "You don't even deserve to be loved in the first place," and no internal monologue or argument could beat that. There was a perverse satisfaction in the certainty of beating myself up in this way. For some reason I liked feeling like I didn't deserve love.

Upon visiting the concentration camps, seeing the spaces people were kept in, tortured in, how no one was provided with any certainty, care, or value, I felt sick. I couldn't fathom that someone would be capable of being that way with another human. It felt like the striving artist way of being, or this inner critic, that had these same uncaring qualities that really didn't give a shit if I died or not since my life had no value in its eyes, came from the same fabric as the Nazi mentality towards the Jews.

After that, it really felt as though I no longer was able to listen or hear the voice. I saw this way of being reflected back in the atrocities and somehow it quieted. At work I had frequently felt burnt out, disconnected from myself, and in a perpetual state of stress throughout my day. I spent a lot of my free time distracting myself from the unease and keeping busy so as to not check in with how uncomfortable I was feeling.

The shift has been away from a voice of persistent negativity, self-shame, and bullying toward existing. It has left a space inside of me, a space that feels neutral, neither positive nor negative. This quiet space in me does allow for room for self-care and attention to my needs. It leaves a space in me for the Buddha Heart when it warms up. Before, this tenderness simply could not exist as it was fuel for the demanding artist. The demanding artist would bully that tenderness.

I know this shift has occurred because in moments of rest and quiet there isn't a flood of negative self-talk happening. When I do feel a questioning of myself, it comes from a place of curiosity, not condemning. Previously, this negativity was ceaseless. I feel more warmth in my chest and a tenderness and a subtle willingness to be touched throughout my day. I notice it often when I walk through the fields to school in the morning by myself. I also notice it at times with students, but more often when I am not in a direct teaching role or with the whole class. I feel it the most with others when we are being authentic and when I am really listening and not just trying to add the next sentence to a conversation. I feel it too when others share how they are experiencing me.

This isn't a permanent state, but when I am not in it I notice the contrast more. When I am not as open to being touched, I become very aware of it and have a desire to be more open, although I have a small concern that I want to make the situation something it is not. I feel like there is some fresh air to this. It feels like this shift has allowed me to shake off the shit I was carrying and instead of experiencing life through a filter that wasn't serving me, I can relate to the world through a new way that feels like it is feeding me, rather than taking from me.

Healing does feel like a transformation to recognizing my wholeness, not just with the world outside of myself, but to make space for all of the competing and conflicting parts within myself. That acknowledgment and recognition of these various parts has taken away a lot of their power and control over me.

This healing has felt like a letting go of something that I couldn't "over-come." I didn't need to beat it, I just needed to let it go.

It also doesn't mean the pain I felt wasn't real or that I need to ignore it. Rather, I accept that it wasn't healthy or serving me, but has led me to this place where I am clear on not wanting to feed it anymore.

I feel an appreciation for you and that I was able to work through this alongside someone else. It makes me feel cared for to have someone else coach me towards feeling love for myself. It makes me feel the love that we have out in the world for others."

COMPLETION OF COACHING

At the point that Martin was completing his coaching program, one of his last assignments was to review his healing narrative and sum up where he is today in his healing journey. Below are his summary points, written in his own words, shared at the completion of coaching.

The inner critic is gone now, or at the very least remains quieted. No longer do the berating and accusations of not deserving love exist. In their place is a space. It doesn't necessarily feel full of love, but rather like a neutral space where love can foster and develop if allowed to.

I feel a wider range of feelings are opening to me, both in terms of deeper love, care, and compassion... yet also for a sharper pain, unease, and acceptance of suffering in life.

I feel less of a fluctuation between feeling isolated and connected to the universe. I feel a growing awareness of connection in my experience of the world, others, and life (although with others is still the trickiest). It feels like in most moments there is at least a glimmer of remembrance that I am a part of the universe, not isolated from it.

I am aware of just how different my life feels looking back through this narrative today. For me it is painful to look back at how much criticism and self-hatred was stirring in my body yet I still felt like such a peaceful guy.

I am also more aware now how my relationship to my body was one that lacked care. Even my exercising and health-related pursuits had an underlying desire to punish me with difficult workouts, feeling the stiffness and discomfort the next day, and feeling I always needed to increase the intensity or weight loads. This of course also brought with it a never-ending feeling of needing to do more than I can, eat better, workout more, see more dramatic results in my body.

Now I am desiring a health plan that works around being caring towards my body and nurturing of it, rather than pushing it and demanding results from it."

CASE STUDY 4: STEP BY STEP BY STEP
John Stoddart, Coach

Rick is in transition. As an elite athlete in his mid-thirties he's actively expanding his career, offering yoga, online education, and coaching. He's in a period of radical change that requires new skills and a shift in perspective towards his public image, his sport, and his identity.

A major health issue is creeping up on him, demanding he assess his priorities around health, family, and relationships. An unsettling diagnosis reveals an incurable, but potentially surgically correctable condition called achalasia, a paralysis of the esophagus limiting his ability to swallow. Rick's self-image of physical mastery is breaking down, and he can no longer deny his need for self-care skills beyond anything his sport ever required of him.

Through our initial coaching conversations, it becomes clear that Rick wants to heal (or fix) his esophagus, but he also wants to use these potent circumstances to develop as a human being, specifically to grow his capacity to be more open and authentic with the people in his life. We are fellow coaches. We share a passion and belief in our methods and we share the nuanced and robust language of our craft. Together we draft the wording for his coaching topic: "to develop my ability to use my symptoms of achalasia to grow and learn relationally, such that I am better able to discover and create my next healing moment with alacrity and passion."

Developing one's ability to heal is a fuzzy concept for Rick as is the idea of a direct link between developing healing capabilities and developing skills in other areas of one's life. Even so, we set about with confidence, drawing upon Rick's lifelong discipline of training, his ability to take on an intense regimen, and his tremendous somatic skills.

We catch ourselves trying to go too deep too fast. Rick isn't responding like an agile athlete. It seems obvious in retrospect that his ability to train physically might not automatically translate into learning to skillfully face a debilitating illness. I'm reminded once again of the incremental nature of our healing journeys. Changing beliefs and shifting everyday patterns takes time, so we slow down dramatically and focus on incrementally developing self-observation skills. Rick gradually builds his awareness of his highly tuned performance skills and his tendency to hide his authentic self behind a public image. Only after he is able to catch himself operating in these ways and begin to relax is he able to attend to the development of new skills.

A professional mountain biker, Rick is used to operating as a self-creator. He's focused and disciplined, constantly challenging himself to move forward rapidly and to achieve immediate results. He has a big following, but even though he operates in a world of many people, he does so alone. He is a lone performer with a deep sense of responsibility to give fully of himself to his fans. He also carries a sense of obligation—to himself, his family, his sponsors, and his public—to perform extraordinary physical feats and to do so consistently. Rick's current way metaphor becomes the Generous Lone Wolf.

The Lone Wolf doesn't like drawing attention to himself unless he's performing on a bike. To get in close, be vulnerable, need help, even share what he's experiencing with achalasia is too self-serving, too self-centered. To Rick, it's selfish. He genuinely and generously puts himself second to the needs of everyone around him, even his audience, not just to control his image or guard his privacy, but to not take up others' time with his troubles. The Lone Wolf is an expert at focusing outward, deflecting attention from himself, blending in. He focuses on the short view. Achalasia is quite a disruption for him.

Though he is drawn instinctively to this deep healing work, he isn't able to articulate exactly why or to engage it with the patient inching-along that's needed to adjust to new and subtle insights. He doesn't know how to read the signs and symptoms. He's not comfortable with mystery and the impreciseness of his situation. Looking after himself has always meant looking after his body in basic ways: physical training, healthy diet, core strength, flexibility, stamina, and coordination. His body has always responded as demanded. Now that something different is being called for, how is he to find his way—to look after himself? His new way metaphor becomes the Openhearted Wayfinder.

The Wayfinder is a seafaring navigator who guides his people across vast oceanscapes without instruments. His precision and confidence are different than the Lone Wolf's. He sees the world as a boundless and mysterious benefactor, all its bits and pieces in a constant process of relational integration. He reads his inner and outer environments looking for information and sensations that he can use to determine his next step along the path. Where the Lone Wolf skirts the periphery, staying separate and alert, the Wayfinder looks to the arc of the horizon, attunes himself to the rhythms of weather and waves—the signs and symptoms—and intuits his course. He takes the long view in space and time. Integration, within himself, with his environment, and with everyone in his sphere, motivates his every move.

Two Developmental Objectives direct the evolution of the Generous Lone Wolf toward the Openhearted Wayfinder:

1. The Tao of Self Care: To develop the ability to accurately navigate masculine and feminine harmony. This involves learning how to stand down the Lone Wolf's generous alpha role while allowing more openhearted exploration of new inner and outer

territory. The benefit of this development is a bigger vision of how to look after Rick. You will learn to more consistently engage your inner healer, which is the ultimate in caring for yourself. In precise terms: bring in your feminine side; get the masculine and feminine flowing together; balance self-doing with self-caring.

2. Opening Your Heart Chakra: To develop the ability to retrain your heart to stay open in the face of physical and emotional distress. Exploring new territory can be exciting, scary, and complex. Achalasia, paralysis in the realm of your heart chakra, can be like a constantly changing seascape with an unforeseeable horizon. Opening your heart chakra encourages the free flow of energy, beliefs, intentions, thoughts, emotions, and affirmations, all part of the Openhearted Wayfinder's navigation towards his destination of healing.

A key piece of navigational information arises in early conversations. Rick shares that he was adopted at birth. This offers insight into the way the Lone Wolf leads his life, as well as providing thrust to Rick's developmental path. We explore how the Lone Wolf relates to not knowing his birth parents, to being separated from this first primal relationship. The Lone Wolf tends to be guided by the immediacy of the facts, such as the loving and healthy nature of his adopted family. Filling in the blanks of time past is secondary to honoring the current circumstances and living his life as it is now and on his own terms. But the mystery is becoming more potent, more relevant as a factor in both Rick's growth and for knowing his health history. What is the healing move to make? It's not a simple question.

Rick's Healing Narrative

Achalasia does not fit with my sense of self. I am a healthy, fit, strong, independent self-made individual. So I assumed these strange symptoms I'm having will quickly pass, just like a common cold. Ignore them until they go away. And thus begins my healing journey ...

Let me start at the beginning. I was adopted and had a wonderful childhood. My parents were supportive and loving and allowed me the flexibility to pursue an alternative and, what turned out to be, a successful career as a professional mountain biker.

For 36 years I had no reason to search for my birth parents. In fact, even after my coaching training to learn to "look-as"—see through another's eyes—I never took my birth parents' perspectives. I never even entertained the thought. As far as I was concerned, I just showed up in the world magically!

So why have I spent the bulk of my life taking risks? Because it makes me feel alive. Why have I nurtured my public persona carefully to become a well-known and liked figure in the cycling world? Because it makes me someone. But how can I feel alive and be someone who just magically showed up in this world? I had to come from somewhere ..."

I'm struck by the potential of Rick exploring his origins. This is a course of action that the Lone Wolf has not been able to take. Is finding his birth parents what Rick wants? How would he prepare for this? What skills does he need in order to make a clear choice, to determine his destination, and choose his course? These questions inform many conversations to come. An early practice is to explore his genetic family by having his DNA analyzed. He begins to relate to the lineage of his bloodline back through time and a felt sense of belonging begins to emerge.

A second navigational point comes to light. Rick has only explored a mainstream medical model for diagnosis and treatment of achalasia. We talk about the Lone Wolf's tendency to limit his focus, deal with only the most pertinent information, and choose a path that keeps everything in sight. What would happen if Rick were to begin to expand his field of view? Collect more information? Ask for feedback and opinions? And develop a wider circle of support? These are all aspects of a richly connected life, fundamental to his coaching topic. We begin with practices that explore his relationship with his inner physical and emotional self.

Rick Healing Narrative Continued

At first, I thought I was having GERD (acid reflux). However, symptoms didn't quite line up. My mysterious symptoms evolved and eventually led me a year later to a specialist. He diagnosed me with achalasia and said my symptoms have no known cause or cure. Kind of like me, I had no known cause or origin, so forget about a cure.

I had to wrestle with the fact that there is something fundamentally wrong with me. What role did I have in creating this? The tension between my sense of self and my symptoms naturally led me to further ignore, shut down inquiry, and learn to live and adapt to symptoms. However, my coach gently inspired me to explore the meaning behind my symptoms, and seek alternative healing modalities."

An Intimate Relationship with Self

The surgical remedy for achalasia requires permanently tearing the tissue to override the paralysis. Rick was deeply touched when I asked him to sit for a few moments and have a quiet conversation with his ailing esophagus. He's not used to relating to his physical body in this way, especially its inner workings. Calling upon his generous nature, he touches into the area that's in distress and he begins to feel for the wellbeing of his body in a new way. His esophagus is no longer an uncooperative and annoying part that needs fixing. His ability or inability to swallow becomes less a mechanical process and more a vital and integral part of the system of his whole being.

Over time, Rick learns to draw more and more upon this inner relationship. He tracks the ebb and flow of his symptoms. He speaks more openly and fully with family, friends, and doctors. He shares his vulnerability on behalf of his body-mind-spirit wellbeing. He watches the horizon for new possibilities, new ideas. He dwells more and more in his potential to change. And he chooses to postpone any medical procedure, allowing time to explore new healing territory.

We underpin Rick's development process with an ongoing qigong practice called the microcosmic orbit. It requires tuning into qi, subtle life energy, directing its flow up the spine to the crown and down the body, around and around through each of the energy chakras. We create more and more ways for Rick to engage the orbit, while he's training, showering, eating, and when awakened in the night by choking. It helps him learn to focus within himself at the same time as it moves dynamic energy through the paralyzed tissue. It encourages the unity of parts and it supports Rick to learn to open his heart at those times when he clenches with fear in reaction to his symptoms. He begins to notice shifts within his physical and emotional self. Symptoms are not resolving, but they are also not quite so fixed in place. Is it possible to mitigate or better manage symptoms? Is it possible to retrain the signaling and integrity of the paralyzed tissue and to encourage fuller function?

Energy flow supports the intertwining and balancing of the masculine and feminine. The Lone Wolf defaults to the outward masculine thrust of life and is disinclined to pause and to nurture himself. He's inclined to fix and move on rather than embrace the multiple elements and the process needed to heal. Rick begins to identify his beliefs and behaviors that restrict his feminine self. He learns gradually to feel the infinite movement between feminine and masculine. As this embodiment gains momentum Rick is able to more readily and more comfortably turn his focus outward. By entering into partnership, his masculine and feminine support greater resilience, courage, patience, sensitivity, and curiosity. All of these are qualities of the Openhearted Wayfinder.

I ask Rick to go back through time, to imagine himself a baby in the arms of his birth mother. Can he feel his mother's heart, her thoughts, her creative spirit? Can he imagine her giving birth knowing that she must let him go? Can he feel his first, most essential relationship being physically severed? Can he feel the unbreakable link that still exists?

Rick Healing Narrative Continued

Am I actually an independent being? Am I a self-made man? Maybe it's more complex than that. I oscillate between training hard, pushing my edges, and submitting to my meaningless symptoms. Though for some reason there was faint curiosity about my birth mother linked to my symptoms. My coach helped me voice this intuition, thus attaching some meaning and reason for my symptoms, as illogical as that sounded to my strong linear and logically thinking mind. So he slowly helped me begin exploring my heritage, first through a DNA test, and eventually by registering with the BC Adoption agency.

I like to be in control. The foundation of my career is about control over my bike, my body, and my image. I have no control over who my birth mother is. It's interesting that I'm willing to take calculated risks on my bike doing tricks and stunts, but when it comes to knowing my birth mother, I'm scared. I'm not in control of the outcome. It's a mystery.

A PASSIONATE RELATIONSHIP WITH THE WORLD

At first his awareness of change needs to be prompted; then Rick begins to notice, more and more on his own, a day-to-day co-existence of the Generous Lone Wolf and the Openhearted Wayfinder. Subtle shifts accumulate and lead to new thoughts, feelings, and actions beyond the Lone Wolf's natural patterns. Rick touches ever more deeply into inner territory and begins to use his senses to navigate. A new value of responsibility to his wellbeing necessitates and inspires connection with others. The liveliness he brings to his sport now flows more easily into his interpersonal life. He bestows kindness more often upon himself. He readily notices distinctions between aspects of the Lone Wolf and the Wayfinder such as generosity, devotion, and discipline. These qualities begin to bridge the transformative process, becoming something different, more well-rounded, through the Wayfinder's expression.

Rick has a distinct sense of healing even as his symptoms continue. He is seeing the gift of illness, and he's much more open to sharing his experience with others, integrating rather than hiding it. He becomes entranced with the journey, more curious than cautious. His birth mother, already registered with the government adoption agency, has been waiting for when he might take the step to connect. He finds a whole new world ready to open to him. Rick's Openhearted Wayfinder is discovering that there is a wide expanse of rich, uncharted territory to explore.

Case Study Five: Liberating Paralyzing Internal Blocks
Amy Phillips, Coach

In some fashion, all coaching topics are healing topics. Alex didn't have an illness per se, but like many people, she was suffering and looked to coaching to alleviate at least some of that suffering. Forty-eight years old, married with a ten- and a five-year-old, Alex absolutely knew she had to make some changes.

She described her topic as: I need to start putting my fiction work out. For the past twenty-five years she had completed a novel every four years. Not one was ever submitted for publication. She found the word submit abhorrent. Now, in the final semester of a two-year MFA program, her sixth novel was her thesis. She owed it to herself to share this one with the world. Until now, she had only shared her work with advisors and fellow writers.

During our Intake conversation, Alex was struck by the parallels we unearthed between holding back her work and holding herself back from others.

Offer conversation: Alex's powers of observation were hard at work when we met three weeks later: "I worry that I've offended people, that I've done something wrong; that it's my fault." She gauged this by how quickly others did or did not respond.

We revised her topic: to build my capacity to share myself, and my work, with the world.

I offered her my sense of her current way of being: the Way of the Undercover Detective" (UD). She laughed and shared her love for this 1940s genre. Her response to the undercover part was more serious: "it's dangerous being undercover, if you get found out." She shared that not only was this image apropos for an observant writer, but that throughout her life she always needed to know where the exits were and what she would do if things suddenly fell apart. We reviewed what the UD had allowed for, such as her keen writer's eye and insatiable curiosity. We then discussed what it closed down. Most obvious was her tendency to withhold herself and her work from others; less obvious was the toll this vigilance was taking on her body. She was tired of living with an "Am I in trouble?" attitude.

I proposed the Way of the Expressive Willow (EW) as her new way of being. This image surprised her and she loved it. I explained that willows are amazingly resilient with enormous root systems, flexible branches, and many healing and magical properties. She saw a real productive and nurturing aspect to the willow, with its long flowing branches and protective space underneath. I suggested that embodying this EW might allow for staying grounded amid anxiety and receiving support from others and the earth. She added to this a deep desire to be of service to her children and others she had not met yet.

We agreed on these developmental objectives:

- You develop more ability to express your authentic voice into the world.
- You develop more ability to observe your fear of moving forward while still taking action on your own behalf.
- You develop more faith in yourself and the people and structures that hold you.

Her self-observation exercise (SOE) entitled Why Not Deeper Connection? encouraged her to notice when the Undercover Detective made a case for avoiding a deeper connection.

For her foundation practice, she agreed to half-hour walks two to three times each week, ideally in nature, paying particular attention to trees she wandered past and aligning with their strength and solidness. Alex left the session appreciative and enthusiastic.

First cycle of development: Alex informed me by email that the SOE had been difficult. She'd discovered an internal critic and realized she projected much of her negativity and fears onto others. She saw and was shocked by how this impacted her ability to stay connected with herself, others, and her work. She shared these painful learnings with her husband and asked if he was interested in a deeper connection. He was interested. She would never have entered into this dialogue in the past and was pleasantly surprised by her willow expressiveness. She was also more forthcoming with her eldest daughter, whom she had stopped singing lullabies to when her youngest was born. She asked if she wanted to be sung to and her daughter replied, "Yes, every second night, please," and so it was.

I encouraged Alex to sing to her own little inner girl, and she was touched by that suggestion.

We reviewed her next practice, Going Under the Radar, in which she looked for the Undercover Detective's ability to sense danger emerging, and when it did, to bring her focus into her body, plant her feet, clasp both hands behind her back, and breathe deeply into her belly. While this surveillance system existed in order to maintain safety, we were not exactly sure what the UD was guarding against. As always, reflective questions accompanied the practice.

Second cycle of development: Alex arrived fresh and eager to share her experience. The practice had been fruitful and challenging. The response from her advisor about her thesis took about three days longer than she'd anticipated. Although she wrote two emails, she didn't send either, despite two anxiety-ridden and sleepless nights. The UDs need to avoid expressing vulnerability was becoming increasingly clear to her.

She began to notice energy showing up in various parts of her body: heart angst when waiting to learn about her work; gut-based when surveying the terrain for danger; and full-body flooding amid real danger (one instance, raccoons). Alex discovered a grove of willow trees en route to her new yoga class—coincidence? Yoga was becoming a mainstay and she was actually craving the opportunity to slow down—and stop!

Eckhart Tolle's *The Power of Now* offered further support, suggesting that more than 80 percent of her high-alert triggers were her own thoughts, primarily future-based, and relating to her fear of being judged.

Alex's next practice, entitled Examining Current Operating Procedures, focused on these future-based fears. She stayed alert for the UDs, making negative assumptions about something that had not yet actually happened, and when she caught herself in the act, she put her hand on her heart and sent it loving energy.

It was wonderful seeing Alex so much gentler with herself—a big shift from the self-loathing (her words) she'd described earlier. She was enjoying including her young self in lullaby time with her daughters, and even sang a little for me—the Expressive Willow in action!

Third cycle of development: Alex continued to both blossom and engage challenges. She found placing hand on heart and sending compassion there provided effective physical and emotional release. It helped illuminate her near constant expectation of being scolded and reduced time spent wallowing in fear. Two situations helped further illuminate this pattern and challenged the Undercover Detective's default position that the world was a hostile place: once with her advisor and once with a classmate; when she asked herself, "Can I trust this person?" She realized the answer was yes—a big breakthrough.

She also realized that she linked worry with success: worry led her to work hard, which led to success. We discussed the benefits of unlinking this dynamic, especially with regard to her upcoming MFA presentation.

She reported several deeply distressing days when the hand-on-heart exercise seemed to fall short, but she stayed with it. Ultimately it was trees that helped her, when she saw that no tree was less a tree even if it was small and stunted. "There are no perfect trees, and they are all perfect trees" (her words). She realized it wasn't she who provided the energy of love and compassion that helped all things grow—it was that thing (or the River of Light as she came to call it). This whole exchange brought tears to my eyes, which she loved!

She had one more bout of being gripped by the pain body (as Tolle calls it), that felt very much like an addiction to her. She didn't even WANT to do hand-on-heart. She wanted to stay miserable and was dumbfounded by that. We spoke about the strength of well-established muscles and the pushback that happens when we challenge the status quo, and the requirement to be gentle with ourselves (and others!) as we experience this.

Alex's work with trustworthiness led us to her next practice, Taking Positive Action, which asked her to stay alert for the UDs withholding information, about work, herself, a situation, etc., whether in the moment or premeditated, like emails that didn't get sent. When she recognized this she was to stop, take a deep breath, and then take action on the Expressive Willow's behalf. She expressed anxiety about her ability to discern "right action," but this abated as we reviewed the spectrum of what this could look like. Her fear also afforded us an opportunity to review how the muscle-building process works. She was intrigued by the notion that all muscles, not just physical, are strengthened in the same way, by systematically exerting them beyond their current limits and then allowing for adequate recovery.

Fourth cycle of development: Alex reported on noticing when she was withholding and taking action anyway. She discovered layers to this dynamic, the most profound being with her mother. In the past she would have never shared her writing with her mother because she was afraid that she would alter it due to her mother's comments. When Alex's mother asked to read her thesis, Alex decided to work with her vulnerability and agreed. She delayed actually handing over the draft and recognized this subtle withholding. When her mother did make critical comments, Alex could see that it wasn't about the work, but about her mother and how she interacted with the work. This breakthrough left her feeling both sad and liberated: sad, seeing her mother's self-centeredness; and liberated, now, imagining sending her work out and differentiating honest critiques from personal agendas. I acknowledged Alex for going through a certain Rite of Passage with her work and her mother. She had gone to deep roots, to the most vulnerable place she could, and instead of recrimination, found freedom and a level of compassion for her mother that she had never known before.

We agreed that negative thoughts would be the next focus for the Expressive Willow during her upcoming MFA residency. Alex offered a recent thought that we decided to work with. We named the practice Compassionate Curiosity and asked her to stay alert for her internal self-talks becoming accusatory, mean, or judgmental (e.g., Why did I do that? Why didn't I do that? She shouldn't have done that!). As soon as she noticed this dynamic she was to STOP what she was doing, close her eyes, and reframe the statement or question as follows:

Ask the question with genuine curiosity. When we are curious, we admit we don't know the answer, but remain open to possibilities. Our mind is not made up. We want to learn.

Ask the question compassionately, with a commitment to one's psychological and spiritual growth and without blame and accusation. The answer helps us grow and develop.

Avoid making yourself wrong when you lack compassion for self or others. Just notice and watch the lack, the difficulty you have generating compassion. In that space of watching, the compassion may arise. You don't have to make it happen.

She left excited and feeling acknowledged. I was left feeling humbled at her progress and grateful to be on this journey with her.

Fifth cycle of development: When Alex returned from her residency, she couldn't wait to share her good news about the practice. She discovered a deep desire to connect with others and realized that virtually 100 percent of the time, her self-criticism arose from judging her desire to connect with others, whether or not she actually connected. She realized that the hyper-vigilant Undercover Detective's approach to relationships allowed little space for actual connection and recognizing that connection was what she wanted, the Expressive Willow ran with it. The ten-day residency was an ideal opportunity to practice these new muscles, and she connected with more people and went deeper into conversations than the UD would have allowed. She described her experience as having beginner's mind, open to what arises with compassionate curiosity. When critical thoughts arose she caught them more easily and forgave herself more readily.

We reviewed Alex's 'core gems,' those qualities or values that are essential for the Expressive Willow's continuing growth and flourishing: her vision, persistence, and belief that anything is possible. The Expressive Willow worked with people and collaborated freely—exactly what Alex had experienced in her residency. This allowed for roominess, flexibility, and an ability to move, unlike the UD's hyper-vigilant tendency toward doom, which felt contracted, rigid, and static: "I might have to learn how to move, but I have the wherewithal." Our conversation illuminated how much Alex already embodied the Expressive Willow, and when I pointed that out, her eyes filled with tears, which she said were based in Joy.

Her final focus practice was entitled Pulling it all Together and I asked her to respond to several questions. The following are the questions and excerpted answers.

How far did I get with each of my developmental objectives?

1. You develop more ability to express your authentic voice into the world.

    [In terms of] my authentic voice as a writer ... I can share my writing now. It's not literally autobiographical ... but it is a reflection of my inner life. So, I was able to give my mother my thesis to read and was able to understand her reaction, not as personal criticism but as evidence of how she is. I was able to read sections of my novel to my brother, sister, kids, husband, and a room full of people in my presentation for my MFA. I also gave the first 120 pages of my novel to four people in my writing group and used the focus practice to get myself through the process. I was able to face the revisions and separate the work from the worry about being critiqued. All this since October! I am looking forward to taking the steps toward publication. So that's a pretty thorough turnaround with sharing my writing. Up until now, the only people who've read or heard my writing were other students or teachers of writing.

    For expressing my own personal (non-writing) voice, I am much more tolerant and compassionate toward myself. I don't feel like I need to be perfect, so I can reveal more of myself, which allows for deeper connections with other people. I realized not everyone is judging me the way I have been judging myself for the past forty years. It is hard to express yourself authentically when you are in a state of more-or-less perpetual self-loathing. I realized that when I couldn't take the self-loathing any more, I turned it outward to other people in the form of contempt or anger. Even if I didn't express my negative judgments openly, this vibe made it hard for other people to trust me, I think.

2. You develop more ability to observe your fear of moving forward while still taking action on your own behalf.

    I was able to see how much I project into the future and how I had the long-standing habit of linking worry to success. My previous mental path was worry=work=success. Now I see it as work=success; the worry is not productive or necessary. I'm still getting a handle on this. My fear of moving forward seemed to come from my fear of being found sub-par or of not measuring up. I always felt judged ever since I was a kid. As a result, I had taken more steps to succeed in "safer" areas like project management—less risky than writing. It does astound me how much writing I did over the past twenty years and how hard I kept trying, considering how loaded failure was for me.

    What I discovered was that with writing, I was so used to thinking of myself as persistent but unsuccessful, that I had managed to just take joy in the process and didn't worry about the outcome. In a way, that looser attitude spread from the writing outward. I also started reading Eckhart Tolle's, The Power of Now *and became aware that my thoughts are not necessarily helpful, that the brain is not always my friend, and I was able to sense a river of light or some kind of spiritual flow inside me, where I could drop those thoughts and experience joy. Emotions usually eluded me in the past. I find*

I'm much more able to laugh or cry now. I remember many occasions as a kid in my bedroom, overwhelmed by emotional pain, crying so hard, but never letting anyone see me. I guess fear of unmanageable emotions recurring led me to avoid them.

3. You develop more faith in yourself and the people and structures that hold you.

   I now have confidence in myself, which has never been the case before, though that's not obvious when people meet me. Even my husband probably never knew I lacked self-confidence. Now, the self-loathing is gone. As soon as I became aware of it, it started to dissipate. I guess I believe in myself now, as a person and as a writer. I've known people who believe in themselves (like my husband), and I've always wondered where they get this confidence. Now I think we're all born with it and some of us lose it, rather than the other way around. Aside from confidence in my writing—not so much my ability to write well, as my ability to see the world a certain way, write imaginary situations, then revise until it's a good read—is my confidence in my own right to exist, to have needs and wants and feelings, and to be able to express myself without feeling bad. This makes interactions with others easier. Also it gives me hope that it's not too late for me to help my kids believe in themselves.

What does this expanded view allow for that wasn't available previously?

   Joy and a more lasting sense of accomplishment as things come to fruition. So I can relax and appreciate how far I've come and look forward with curiosity to what's still to come. I need these new abilities for my writing, to do justice to the story I'm trying to tell.

What skills do I have that will support me to continue stabilizing and growing more fully into the Expressive Willow?

> *I can see my undercover detective skills continuing to be useful in life—observation, curiosity, vigilance, work ethic, etc. These can develop in new directions, complemented with compassion, roots, taking care of myself with walks and yoga, believing in myself. Eventually, I can see how ongoing development, spiritually and emotionally, will influence every aspect of my life and be a powerful example to my daughters, who are just starting to experience the world. I want them to have the sense of joy I've found. I feel I will be much more ready for death when it comes. The patience I've shown to my writing has extended to other parts of my life. Maybe I can help new writers of any age at some point. I don't see any limits to this growth."*

How do I see life differently in light of all that I've achieved?

> *I have experienced a profound lightening of spirit. Wow! I am so happy for me, my family, and my friends, too, but especially my husband and children. Everything is better.*

Completion: This was a wonderful opportunity for us to look at Alex's steady headway throughout the coaching relationship, from the Offer session (when she declared that she thought this was going to change her life), through the painful realizations that emerged during the SOE, and culminating in our last session when she shared her amazingly "expressive" experience in her residency.

We were both gratified to see how much progress she had made with her developmental objectives. She intended to stay with the yoga practice she had come to love as well as with the compassionate curiosity practice. In fact, compassion was another core gem that she identified. She was working full-time on her novel and was grateful to have had this coaching experience that opened her heart. She had her stable of "doulas" around her, writing friends who were prepared to help her "birth this baby" by critiquing her novel when she was ready. She couldn't imagine NOT sending this work out for publication, a far cry from barely tolerating the word submit!

We agreed to meet in a month for a check-in, my gift to her, but also a gift to me. This woman was truly an inspiration and I feel so very blessed to have played a part in bringing her work and her voice forward in the world. I acknowledged her courage, her commitment, and her generosity of spirit. She has been in my corner every bit as much as I have been in hers.

REFLECTING ON FIVE CASE STUDIES—WE JUST NEVER KNOW

The authors are pleased, and not surprised, that these five case studies have manifested in the distinct voices and narrative styles of the coaches who lived them. Healing through coaching cannot be a one- or even some-size-fits-all practice.

A woman diagnosed with multiple sclerosis lives ever-more-deeply into a healthy life with her family and writing; a man with chronic fatigue discovers his own concern with "what should be" is an underlying catalyst, if not *the* cause of his exhaustion; an elite athlete transforms his relationship with his body and his sense of identity as he negotiates a condition that thwarts his digestion; a man with a deep sense of self-hatred and low self-worth grows into an acceptance of who he is and his value as a human being; and a writer afraid to submit her work to the world learns to open herself to family and friends, and the writing is set free as well.

We don't know—*can't* know—at the beginning of a coaching relationship where we will go with our client. We trust our training, skills, and desire to serve. We trust the client's commitment to do the work that healing requires, and we begin. What one of our colleagues engages in his yoga practice, seems to fit our coaching as well: In any given moment, as coach or client, we can choose to give our attention to *skillful means*—whatever that might mean—from noticing our posture and breath, to taking a nap, to taking the next step on our journey; or to *a sense of ease*—exploring how we can live right now with less struggle; or to *befriending everything that arises*, letting go our resistance to, and inviting, life, as Rumi encourages us in "The Guest House"; and to Mystery, acknowledging and embracing what is currently beyond our capacity to understand. In this manner, we move in a dance with our clients, uncovering what is unseen for them and co-creating a new and more supportive way of being in the world.

Healing Means Befriending Everything

—Leslie Williams

"You can't be sick. You look like the picture of health."

"Um, thank you?"

"How have you brought this on yourself? What part of you wants this?"

"Um, screw you."

"I can see that you're crying. I don't think you're sick. I think you're depressed."

"You try this life on and let me know how happy you feel."

"Here's the number of a great trainer. She will totally kick your ass, which is exactly what you need."

"Did you bother to ask about the time a gentle yoga class put me in bed for five weeks?"

What these people see is a slug. Someone overweight and out of shape. Someone who cancels out of things at the last minute. Someone well-meaning but unreliable. Maybe even lazy.

What they don't see is who's been lost. They don't see the high-schooler who always skipped lunch to shoot hoops with the boys. They don't see the adult who played paddle tennis every Monday night in the freezing cold or the one who boogied all night and woke up the next morning, rarin' to go.

What they don't see is the person whose greatest joy and sense of mastery used to come through the life of the body. Today, that person is totally out of reach.

My chronic energy deficit began suddenly one day, the day I came out of my fourth knee surgery to fix sports injuries. After the first three surgeries, I rehabbed like a champ. I brought my signature competitiveness, drive, and love of physical challenge.

But the fourth surgery was different. I wasn't "coming back" like I had. It felt like I had left some life force on the surgeon's table. When I was in rehab after number four, I could do only the barest minimum of exercises and fell in a heap after just a few minutes of exertion.

Overnight, I became less: diminished, like a faded photograph. And I still don't know why. This has been my form of illness for 20 years now. It's not tragic or dramatic, but it is nonetheless difficult. It doesn't "show," so people are confused. There's nothing to vanquish, no concrete diagnosis to rally around. With no cure available, I've realized that I must somehow befriend this invisible companion that I never saw coming and that I can't evict through effort or diligence.

It's meant learning to relate to my condition and my life with kindness, curiosity, and creativity. This has taken great intention and practice. I'm continually learning to ask for help. To make commitments that are realistic. To strive to remember how harmful it is to "effort" through life. To somehow make peace with the dissonance of housing a wildly alive spirit within this worn-out body. To find eyes for the depth and richness that only a "small" life can reveal.

I'm writing this from the midst of the healing journey, so I don't know how the story goes from here. What I do know, however, is that grace abounds, even when energy is scarce. Tending more to my own "ecology,"

I've become more finely attuned to others. Tuning into the tiny jewels in my small life, my sense of gratitude and wonder intensify. Abandoning my obsession with self-improvement, my humility and compassion deepen.

Whatever happened in that operating room that day 20 years ago, I did not want it and I did not ask for it. But when I can befriend my life as it is, I move—in microns or in miles—toward wholeness. I heal.

∞

Chapter 5

Moving Forward

The potential for wholeness, for health, resides in all of us, as does the potential for illness and disharmony. Disease is disharmony. More accurately, it is an expression of internal disharmony. If illness is seen as foreign and external, we may end up waging a war against ourselves.

—Gabor Maté

Next Steps

What next? As coaches there are several steps that we can take to develop the sensitivity and skill for working with clients with illness and disability. Mostly this involves deepening our relationship with illness and healing. Three accessible methods are:

- Inquiring into our own healing narrative
- Learning more about illness and healing through reading and audio/video resources
- Spending increased time with individuals with illness and pain

The process of understanding a healing narrative is not challenging; it's just not the usual orientation we take about our health.

Notice that when we read a newspaper, a magazine, or online source, or even when we spend time with a healthcare provider, often much of our orientation is on symptoms of illness and what we might do to rid ourselves of these symptoms. The inquiry of a healing narrative asks us to consider what our experience is of healing. What does it feel like? What do we do when we heal? Who is involved with our healing process? What systems support our healing? By continuing to keep the focus on healing rather than on illness, we can identify key elements in our healing. Turning this into a healing narrative is just the final stage in which we write out our healing story. Chapter 2 offers several different types of exercises to choose from to do this inquiry yourself.

Developing a healing vocabulary through reading is essential to working with clients with illness and trauma. A bibliography of books that have been influential in our lives is offered at the end of this book. Some of these titles were read together as a group, while most of us continue to dig deeply into these texts over time. There is no one book that is a must read. Review the bibliography and choose a book that seems to speak directly to you. You'll find most, if not all of the books on our list, will be relevant to you and your clients. Explore the ever-growing audio/video resources that are available as well.

Some of us experience quite a bit of illness in our lives; others do not. As coaches developing our coaching skills, spending time with people in situations in which we can experience first-hand persons living with disease is essential. For some, that might be taking care of a parent or a family member with a chronic complaint. For others it may be a men's or women's group in which pain and suffering are addressed regularly. Still others will have to consciously choose to volunteer in situations that directly offer experience with persons who struggle with their health. The more time we spend with real people, the more our hearts will open and our presence will become sensitive and open to the suffering of others. This is essential development for coaching clients with illness.

As coaches it is essential that we hold the space for healing to occur with our clients. Creating and maintaining a safe container is essential, and is in fact embedded in the coaching relationship. We understand the potential for growth within every moment of a coaching program. A powerful question can change the course of a client's life, and so the opportunity for transformation, for spontaneous healing, is ever-present. We support the client's stepping onto a healing continuum on which incremental shifts, the continuous process of transcending and including, provide him or her the opportunity to learn, over and over, a felt sense of the difference between disintegration and integration. Even with a spontaneous healing moment, when a perspective shift opens up new possibilities, the ripples of change will be ongoing as the embodiment of the client's new way is experienced more fully and deeply over time. Olivia's story is a beautiful illustration of each aspect of this healing trinity. Her new way metaphor, Dorothy and Her Friends, continues to support her healing long after completion with her coach, just as we always hope our clients will continue to experience deeper levels of embodiment of the fruits of the coaching relationship.

Our culture sets us up to want to get better or to be cured, and the opposing forces of defeat and collapse are constant possibilities. In chronic illness states, objectivity intertwines with hope, expectation, and fear. We can help our clients to develop an ability to investigate and challenge these outer and inner forces and to trust that their healing narrative can continue, chapter by chapter. Our clients learn to hold their vulnerable new selves as gently as a newborn while the healing unfolds. As coaches we know this to be the foundation of resilience, a quality that will support a healing journey that lasts a lifetime.

Since we started working on this project, many of us have found our words and stories to be invaluable in new episodes of pain and illness. Relapses of chronic conditions and break-ups of relationships have required us to repeatedly bring our attention to healing. As a collaborative process, our commitment to working together, understanding ourselves and our healing processes, has deepened our ability to feel more fully both the pain and the potential for growth that healing offers. Our hearts have grown closer, experiencing sadness and laughter as one.

Exploring the landscape of this book, keep in mind that coaching offers a well-developed container for working with clients who are in need of healing. This is not in any way a replacement for medical attention. Conventional and integrative medical interventions mostly attend to the medical condition of the patient. Psychiatrists and psychotherapists are trained to work with mental health conditions. We as coaches are not meant to replace any of these health professionals.

Rather, as coaches, our presence, our hearts, and our skills are offered in support of healing for those who make the commitment to working with a coach. Our work is to deepen our ability to be present with the full range of the human condition and to skillfully support the emergence of healing.

Afterword

We have been engaged in a several-year journey to better understand healing from the inside. As we come to the end of this shared journey in print, this guide to coaching and healing is a gathering of what we've learned—when healing from injury, illness, trauma, or loss is central to the coaching program. We have drawn from our experiences as coaches and from our own personal healing journeys.

As authors, we are acutely aware of both our shared coaching method and the expansive and diverse possibilities, beyond any method, toward which an integral approach to coaching and healing beckons. The differentiation of curing and healing, the difference between a disease narrative and a healing narrative, the various approaches to writing a narrative that is truly healing, and the creation and holding of a safe, sacred coaching relationship in which healing can be nurtured, are all essential to this work.

We deeply believe in what we are doing and in how we are doing it. We encourage readers to continue this conversation, among yourselves and with us, in person and online. We invite our coaching colleagues to explore the waters of healing in your practices, and we invite health professionals to explore the benefits of coaching and healing in your crucial conversations with your patients.

Thanks for joining us on the path.

NURSING HOME RETURN

—Reggie Marra

She sits on the veranda
late evening sun
above the Palisades
deepens the soft warm
radiance of her face.

Massaging the swollen left hand
in both of hers
she alternates between
drill sergeant and dutiful
loving daughter
demanding and deferential
always a quick smile ready.

The nursing home conjures
my memories of many wheels
in motion sitting down
and as I watch her love
the hand that held and
loved her earliest moments
the certain uncertainty of
life loss and love surrounds
and supports us.

HEALING IS LOVE

—John Stoddart

What is the biggest picture of healing you can imagine? I have asked myself many times how I can create the most favorable conditions to activate and sustain healing. If I were to choose just one thing, an ultimate healing force, it must be love. Not squishy love. I mean the full-spectrum love of life and self that expands my ability to confront and cope with physical and emotional pain. The kind of love that helps me regrow my resilience and eases the rigidness of anxiety, confusion, and grief that accompany loss of health, loss of any kind.

This kind of big love holds all things in its embrace: the voyage and the destination; the hope, the meaning, the effort, even the suffering itself. Through this love I forgive my failures and my failing body. I am able to wholeheartedly engage the misfortunes and mistreatments of my life. In this love, I transcend denial, fear, and anger and move toward acceptance, and eventually to the hard-won knowledge that illness is, paradoxically, an extraordinary gift. In a "What's Your Tree" circle, we explored life purpose. Mine became: to love myself to death. And so each day I place myself and all my symptoms in the warm glow of this declaration, and I become my own healer.

Healing always comes from within, even when sparked and enabled by someone or something outside of ourselves. We are each our own healer and that deeper well of love is our ultimate healing force. Gary Zukav affirms, "Eventually you will come to understand that love heals everything, and love is all there is." Healing happens with big love and small steps. When we launch military-like campaigns, fight brave battles to defeat the forces of illness, we must be careful that the barricades we create do not separate us from our own healing source. Each day, reminding ourselves that there is, within us, an inner healer, we create a powerful tipping point toward healing.

Appendix One:
Overview of Integral Theory

Every word and sentence we speak, hear, write, or read, every belief or opinion we hold, every issue we face, every occasion that arises in our lives, every "other" with whom we interact exists amid a beautifully elegant and complex array of influences, characteristics, and perspectives. The more deeply we know the lenses, biases, strengths, and blind(ish) spots through which we see, behave, and assess how things are going, the more "accurate" and "intimate" we can be in our lives. An integral perspective helps us toward this end.

What follows is a brief overview of quadrants, levels, lines, states, and types (AQAL). If you would like a more detailed overview, we recommend, *"An Overview of Integral Theory: An All-Inclusive Framework for the 21st Century"* by Sean Esbjörn-Hargens, available online at https://www.integrallife.com/integral-post/overview-integral-theory and/or, *"The Integral Operating System"* by Ken Wilber, at https://www.integrallife.com/integral-post/integral-operating-system.

Quadrants: refer to four perspectives:

1. My beliefs and values—what and how I'm feeling or thinking right now—the *interior* of an *individual* or intention: Upper Left;
2. What we (you and I) believe or agree on—the *interior* of a *collective* or culture: Lower Left;
3. The observable aspects or *exterior* of an *individual* or behavior: Upper Right; and
4. The observable aspects or *exterior* of a *collective* or society: Lower Right.

Other ways to view the quadrants are Beauty (UL), Goodness (LL) and Truth (UR/LR), or Art (UL), Morals (LL) and Science (UR/LR).

Lines: Developmental lines or multiple intelligences (Gardner). While there are many developmental lines, we work with six specific lines/intelligences: cognitive, moral, emotional, interpersonal, somatic, and spiritual. Each line of development represents increasing level of skill in one particular domain.

Levels: The stages or levels that these lines and consciousness "itself" can develop through (a generic example would be growth from ego-centric/me to ethnocentric/us to world-centric/all of us to Kosmos-centric/all that is perspectives; a more practical example would be acorn → seedling → oak tree). Using the work of Ken Wilber, Susanne Cook-Greuter, Robert Kegan, Bill Torbert, Don Beck and others, we look for, attune to, and intuit the developmental "center of gravity" from and through which our clients orient in order to best meet them where and as they are—always aware of the deep humility required in us to work in this way.

INDIVIDUAL	
Upper Left (UL) **Interior Individual** e.g., intention, thought, values beliefs, etc. **1st-person perspective** "I" language Art/Beauty	**(UL) Upper Right** **Exterior Individual** e.g., actions, behaviors, experiences traits, etc. **3rd-person perspective** "it" language Science/Truth
Interior Group/Collective e.g., culture, relationship, *shared* values/beliefs, etc. **2nd-person perspective** "we" language Morals/Goodness Lower Left (LL)	**Exterior Group/Collective** e.g., environment, society, infrastructure, systems, etc. **3rd-person perspective** "its" language Science/Truth (LR) Lower Right
COLLECTIVE	

The left edge of the box is labeled vertically: INTERIOR. The right edge is labeled vertically: EXTERIOR.

States: States of consciousness that are available at any level of development. Four "overarching" states are waking (gross), dreaming (subtle), deep, dreamless sleep (causal), and the dropping of boundaries among these three (nondual); and including non-ordinary states (e.g. drug induced), trained states (e.g. meditative), other, more common day-to-day states like agitated, blissful, equanimous, angry, bored, jealous, for example, and various energetic states such as low, high, resourceful, and unresourceful states.

Types: Aspects of consciousness such as gender and personality that exist at all developmental levels, but that do not themselves measure development. Within each type, development can take place. For examples, each Enneagram type is neither better nor worse, earlier nor later, nor more or less inclusive than any other type, but an individual can inhabit a higher or lower level of development within his or her type; or we do not develop from masculine to feminine, or vice versa; and finaly, ectomorphic, mesomorphic, and endomorphic body types differ, but do not indicate earlier/later or lower/higher development.

Appendix Two:
Integral Coaching—A Potent Path for Healing

Coaching approaches and schools abound; each has its particular strengths and limitations. The authors believe that Integral Coaching Canada's Integral Coaching Method developed by Laura Divine and Joanne Hunt is particularly suited for the healing domain. In this section, we will outline the unique features of the Integral Coaching approach. We believe our learning can inform coaches from all schools in dealing with healing topics. The descriptions that follow, although in our own words, illuminate a few parts of Integral Coaching Canada's work and we thank them for their support in this written capture of our unique experiential journey.

While there are many unique aspects of the Integral Coaching approach, we will highlight three that differentiate this method:

1. Holistic understanding of the client:
    As Integral Coaches we use a holistic approach to gain a broad, precise, and compassionate view of our clients. We see, appreciate, and understand our clients through (at least)

six "lenses." These lenses make up what ICC calls the AQAL Constellation for the client. The lenses are:

a. Quadrants—a map of four universal perspectives on the world. This lens helps us to learn which perspectives most guide our client in navigating his/her situation and which are most missing from his or her view, as well as the competencies available in each quadrant.

b. Lines of Development—a system of six developmental competencies. Understanding the relative strengths and weaknesses of a client helps the coach to understand what skills can be relied on and which need(s) to be strengthened.

c. Embodied Levels of Consciousness—a map of consciousness development. This map helps the coach to identify the relative level of complexity at which a client is capable of operating.

d. States of Consciousness—a lens that helps us key into a client's patterned qualities of being.

e. Types Structures—two different type structures (gender and enneatype) help the coach to see some of the patterned ways in which a client tends to see himself, understand his world, and take action.

2. Developmental approach to change:

The concept of "include and transcend" is foundational to the ICC's Integral Coaching method and process of development. This means that we value the client as she is and work to utilize those parts of herself that support her healing journey.

Yet we also seek to expand upon that so that the client has a wider view and greater skills to support her healing.

We capture the "include and transcend" concept by helping the client to articulate both her Current Way of Being (CWOB) and her New Way of Being" (NWOB). The notion of transcending the CWOB to the NWOB, while including the useful, necessary, and healthy components of the CWOB, is foundational to how we as Integral Coaches approach development. Being able to transcend the dark elements of dis-ease and include the individualized components of joy, love, strength, courage, connection, and more, is what the healing process is all about.

The CWOB is the way a client views the world, checks for affirmation that his/her worldview is correct, and supports or inhibits behavior change based on that view. "The strong 'present' of a CWOB is a comprehensive unification of all past moments, a culmination of who and what we have been up until the current moment. As such, it is important for a developmental system to acknowledge its power and resiliency. The muscles of this CWOB have been uniquely honed to support our current manifestation." (Hunt, pg. 11-12, 2009) This perfectly describes why the client is stuck and in pain—he/she literally cannot see the way out. The ICC's Integral Coaching method uses the terms Way of Seeing, Way of Going, and Way of Checking to describe how a client's CWOB and NWOB manifest in the world.

The NWOB suggests the way the client will develop a new view of the world, will check for affirmation that the view is correct, and will support productive actions based on that view.

It is a view of how the client will be when he/she achieves his/her topic and provides an anchor that the client can use while progressing through the change process. Both the CWOB and NWOB are presented to the client through metaphor. As Robert Kegan states (as cited in Hunt, pg. 78, 2009):

Metaphors. . . have a number of salutary features, especially when they are introduced tentatively, with an ear to the client's own use of images and a readiness to abandon the offered metaphor if the client does not incorporate it into her own discourse. A metaphor is interpretive, but it is an interpretation made in soft clay rather than cold analysis. It invites the client to put his hands on it and reshape it into something more fitting to him. Especially when the therapist's metaphor addresses the internal circumstances of being a maker of meaning-structures, the client may find that, drawn to put his hands to reshaping it, he is engaged in reshaping the very way he knows.

These two metaphors, the Current Way and the New Way, are the bookends that bind and support the coaching journey.

3. Structured method and process for development:

Sustainable development rarely happens by chance or through a series of disconnected conversations. It happens through a well-structured process that guides the client in moving from her CWOB to her NWOB. The coach crafts a targeted program that meets the client where he/she is in his/her journey enabling him/her to make progress within the Coaching Topic. This program creates a systematic process of change, so that in many cases, a healing challenge can underlie the main topic and a capable coach can support healing on many levels as the client evolves through the program. The method includes a four phase process:

a. Intake Conversation: An in-depth conversation where the coach and client establish the coaching topic, and the coach learns about the unique way in which the client currently approaches that issue in her life. The coach uses the lenses comprising a client's AQAL Constellation to guide his/her questions.

b. Offer Conversation: A follow-up conversation where the coach confirms the topic, offers CWOB and NWOB metaphors, works with the client to build final metaphors that land accurately and powerfully, and proposes the major developmental objectives for the program based on what the client shared and was mutually explored during the Intake Conversation.

c. Cycles of Development Conversation: A process of sequenced conversations and practices that grow a client's skill in the Developmental Objectives identified in the formal Coaching Program. Each practice is highly customized for a particular client, within their unique profile, created specifically for the current place in the "include and transcend" change process, that enables them to see more of both the CWOB and NWOB, and is scaled appropriately so that the right degree of change is created: "Through this structured, integral developmental process, the client progressively dis-identifies with their CWOB and shifts their essential identity to the NWOB. They are still able to draw upon the strengths and capacities from their CWOB, but they now do so from the vantage point and capabilities associated with their NWOB." (Hunt, pg. 13, 2009).

d. Completion Conversation: The capstone of the coaching process. In this session, the coach and client register the new capabilities now embodied in the client, anticipate barriers going forward, and construct a set of practices and structures that will allow the client to sustain and continue progress in the healing topic.

For more information about this powerful Integral Coaching method and approach, please go to www.integralcoachingcanada. com, search YouTube for videos of Laura Divine and Joanne Hunt discussing the method, and refer to the Spring 2009 Journal of Integral Theory and Practice which was entirely dedicated to the work of Integral Coaching Canada.

BIBLIOGRAPHY

CANCER

Buckman, R. (2006). *Cancer Is a Word, Not a Sentence: A Practical Guide to Help You Through the First Few Weeks.* Cheektowaga, NY: Firefly Books.

Clifford, C.K. (2011). *Laugh 'Til It Heals: Notes From the World's Funniest Cancer Mailbox.* Tunbridge Wells, England: Anshan Publishers.

Rutledge, R. & Walker, T. (2010). *The Healing Circle: Integrating Science, Wisdom, Compassion in Reclaiming Wholeness on the Cancer Journey.* Montreal, Quebec: Healing and Cancer Foundation.

Servan-Schreiber, D. (2009). *Anti-Cancer: A New Way of Life.* New York, NY: Viking Adult.

CONSCIOUSNESS

Gardner, H. (2011). *Frames of Mind: The Theory of Multiple Intelligence.* New York, NY: Basic Books Inc.

Lipton, B. (2007). T*he Biology of Belief: Unleashing the Power of Consciousness, Matter, & Miracles.* Carlsbad, CA: Hay House.

McCartney, F. (2005). *Body of Health: The New Science of Intuition Medicine for Energy and Balance.* Novato, CA: New World Library.

Myss, C. (2011). *Defy gravity: Healing Beyond the Bounds of Reason.* Carlsbad, CA: Hay House.

Dying

Halifax, J. (2008). *Being With Dying: Cultivating Compassion and Fearlessness in the Presence of Death*. Boulder, CO: Shambhala.

Kuhl, D. (2003). *What Dying People Want: Practical Wisdom for the End of Life*. Jackson, TN: Public Affairs Books.

Levine, S. (1998). *A Year to Live: How to Live This Year as if It Were Your Last*. New York, NY: Bell Tower.

Levine, S. & Levine, O. (2012). *Who Dies? An Investigation of Conscious Living and Conscious Dying*. New York, NY: Random House, LLC.

Wyatt, K.M. (2012). *What Really Matters: Seven Lessons for Living From the Stories of the Dying*. New York, NY: Select Books.

Emotions

Seligman, M. (2006). *Learned Optimism: How to Change Your Mind and Your Life*. London, England: Vintage.

Seligman, M. (2012). *Flourish: A Visionary New Understanding of Happiness and Well-Being*. New York, NY: Atria Books.

Siegel, B. (1998). *Love, Medicine and Miracles: Lessons Learned About Self-Healing from a Surgeon's Experience With Exceptional Patients*. New York, NY: William Morrow Paperbacks.

Grief

Kubler-Ross, E. & Kessler, D. (2005). O*n Grief and Grieving: Finding the Meaning of Grief Through the Five Stages of Loss*. New York, NY: Simon and Schuster.

Healing

Bernhard, T. (2010). *How to Be Sick: A Buddhist-Inspired Guide for the Chronically Ill and Their Caregivers*. Somerville, MA: Wisdom Publications, Inc.

Connelly, D. (1994). *All Sickness is Home Sickness*. Baltimore, MD: Wisdom Well Press.

Cunningham, A. (1994). *The Healing Journey: Overcoming the Crisis of Cancer*. Bolton, ON: Key Porter Books.

Duff, K. (2000). *The Alchemy of Illness*. New York, NY: Harmony.

Edwards, G. (2012). *Conscious Medicine: Creating Health and Well-Being in a Conscious Universe*. London, England: Piatkus Books.

Schlitz, M, & Amorak, T, & Micozzi, M. (2005). *Consciousness and Healing: Integral Approaches to Mind-Body Medicine*. Amsterdam, Netherlands: Elselvier Churchill Livingstone.

LIFESTYLE

Chopra, D. (1994). *Ageless Body, Timeless Mind: The Quantum Alternative to Growing Old*. New York, NY: Three Rivers Press.

Dacher, E. (2006). *Integral Health: The Path to Human Flourishing*. Laguna Beach, CA: Basic Health Publications.

Kabat-Zinn, J. (1990). *Full Catastrophe Living: Using the Wisdom of Your Body and Mind to Face Stress, Pain, and Illness*. Peaslake, Surrey England: Delta.

Leonard, A., Wilber, K. & Patten, T. (2008). *Integral Life Practice: A 21st-Century Blueprint for Physical Health, Emotional Balance, Mental Clarity and Spiritual Awakening*. Boulder, CO: Shambhala.

Leonard, G. & Murphy, M. (1995). *The Life We Are Given: A Long-Term Program for Realizing the Potential of Body, Mind, Heart, and Soul*. New York, NY: G. P. Putnam's Sons.

Shwalbe, W. (2013). *The End of Your Life Book Club*. London, England: Vintage.

NUTRITION

Bauman, E., Waldman, H. & Abrams, D (2012). *The Whole-Food Guide for Breast Cancer Survivors: A Nutritional Approach to Preventing*

Recurrence. Oakland, CA: New Harbinger Publications, Inc.

Beliveau, R. & Gingras, D. (2009). *Eating Well, Living Well: An Everyday Guide for Optimum Health*. Toronto, ON: McClelland & Stewart.

Beliveau, R. & Gingras, D. (2007). *Cooking With Foods That Fight Cancer*. Toronto, ON: McClelland & Stewart.

PAIN

Brand, P. & Yancey, P. (1997). *The Gift of Pain*. Grand Rapids, MI: Zondervan.

Sanford, M. (2008). *Waking: A Memoir of Trauma and Transcendence*. Emmaus, PA: Rodale Books.

Thernstrom, M. (2011). *The Pain Chronicles: Cures, Myths, Mysteries, Prayers, Diaries, Brain Scans, Healing, and the Science of Suffering*. New York, NY: Picador.

POETRY COLLECTIONS

Goldsmith, E. (1997). *No Pine Tree in This Forest is Perfect*. Sleepy Hollow, NY: Slapering Hol Press.

Housden, R. (2003). *Risking Everything: 110 Poems of Love and Revelation*. New York, NY: Harmony.

Housden, R. (2007). *Dancing With Joy: 99 Poems*. New York, NY: Harmony.

Bly, R., Meade, M. & Hillman, J., eds. (1992). *The Rag and Bone Shop of the Heart*. New York, NY: Harper Perennial.

POETRY WRITING

Behn, R. & Twichell, C., eds. (1992). *The Practice of Poetry*. New York, NY: Harper Collins.

Fox, J. (1997). *Poetic Medicine: The Healing Art of Poem-Making*. New York, NY: Tarcher-Putnam.

Goldberg, N. (1990). *Wild Mind: Living the Writer's Life*. New York, NY: Bantam.

Goldberg, N. (1986). *Writing Down the Bones: Freeing the Writer Within*. Boston, MA: Shambhala.

SOMATICS

Caldwell, C. (1996). *Getting Our Bodies Back*. Boulder, CO: Shambhala.

Levine, P. (2010). *In an Unspoken Voice: How the Body Releases Trauma and Restores Goodness*. Berkeley, CA: North Atlantic Books.

Naparstek, B. (2005). *Invisible Heroes: Survivors of Trauma and How They Heal*. New York, NY: Bantam.

SPIRITUALITY

Bedard, J. (1999). *Lotus in the Fire: The Healing Power of Zen*. Boulder, CO: Shambhala.

Bohr, R. (2011). *Falling Upward: A Spirituality for the Two Halves of Life*. Hoboken, NJ: Jossey-Bass.

STRESS

Maté, G. (2011). *When the Body Says No: Exploring the Stress-Disease Connection*. Hoboken, NJ: John Wiley & Sons.

WEBSITES AND DVDS

Mind Body Solutions (Producer) (2009). *Transforming Disability: A Mind Body Approach with Matthew Sanford* [DVD]. United States: Producer.

Carr, K. (2013). *Crazy Sexy Cancer*. Retrieved from http://kriscarr.com/products/crazy-sexy-cancer/

Walker, T. & Beaupre, C. (Producers) (date unknown). *Healing Skills: Qigong, Yoga and Meditation* [DVD]. Canada: Healing and Cancer Foundation

REFERENCES

Antonovsky, A. (1979). *Health, Stress, and Coping*. San Francisco, CA: Jossey-Bass Inc.

Charon, R. (2009). *Narrative Medicine: Honoring the Stories of Illness*. New York, NY: Oxford University Press.

Hunt, J. (2014). Transcending and Including Our Current Way of Being: An Introduction to Integral Coaching Canada, *Journal of Integral Theory and Practice*, 4(1), pp. 1-20

Hunt, J. & Divine, L. (2004). *Certification Module: Program Material and Theory*. Ottawa, Canada: Integral Coaching Canada Inc.

Kleinman, A. (1989). *The Illness Narratives: Suffering, Healing, and the Human Condition*. New York, NY: Basic Books.

Levin, J. (2008). Integrating Positive Psychology into Epidemiologic Theory: Reflections on Love, Salutogenesis, and Determinants of Population Health. In S.G. Post (Ed.), *Altruism and Health* (pp.189-218). New York, NY: Oxford University Press.

Maté, G. (2011). *When the body says no: Exploring the stress-disease connection*. Hoboken, NJ: John Wiley & Sons.

Mehl-Madrona, L. (2007). *Narrative Medicine: The Use of History and Story in the Healing Process*. Rochester, VT: Inner Traditions.

Travis, J & Ryan, RA, (2004). *The Wellness Book: How to Achieve Enduring Health and Vitality*. NY, NY: Ten Speed Press.

Wilber, K (2000). A Brief History of Everything, Boston, MA: Shambala Inc.

Glossary

AQAL Constellation™: Drawing on the powerful Integral framework called AQAL (short for All Quadrants, All Levels, All Lines, All States, All Types) originally proposed by Ken Wilber, when the coach plots where the client falls in each aspect of AQAL, the client's particular patterned way of being is revealed. This pattern is referred to as an AQAL Constellation, and it gives the coach a precise, holistic, and compassionate understanding of each person as a unique individual.

Coaching Program: A coaching program refers both to the written architecture of a coaching engagement and to the developmental process itself. The coaching program outlines the specific coaching goal and supporting developmental objectives, which guide the coach and client throughout the engagement.

Current Way of Being (CWOB): The patterned way in which a client views the world, takes action (or doesn't) as a result of that view, and checks for affirmation that his/her worldview is valid.

Cycle of Development: A cycle of development is a segment of the developmental journey. Each cycle builds upon the previous cycle to form an iterative, staged, and coherent path of growth

Developmental Objective: The two or three major competencies set forth in the coaching program. These objectives serve as the focus of the client's development in a given program.

Focus Practice: The focus practice is an exercise that is designed for the client to carry out for a limited period of time during the coaching program. Each practice is customized for each client. The design is informed by: a) the client's unique profile; b) his/her current place in the change process; and c) the scale which will simultaneously support and stretch him or her so that the right degree of change is created.

Foundation Practice: The foundation practice is a practice that is designed to be carried out for an extended period of time, often for the duration of the program. Whereas the focus practice is designed to build smaller-level capabilities in support of the program goals, the foundation practice is intended to build more fundamental capacity.

Healing Topic: The healing topic sets the foundation for the coaching program. Clients with healing topics have generally suffered some type of trauma: an illness, an injury, or other significant loss.

Include and Transcend: Include and transcend emphasizes that the purpose within our growth and development is not to exclude any knowledge or experience that preceded the current state of understanding, but rather to incorporate it within as a stepping stone to further deepening our perspective. Through its cycles of development the ICC methodology builds the capacities and capabilities to grow into a NWOB while also working to integrate the healthy aspects of our CWOB as we include and transcend it.

Levels of Consciousness: Levels refer to the stages that these developmental lines, and consciousness itself, can develop through. A practical example is acorn → seedling → oak tree. A more technical example is growth from ego-centric/me to ethnocentric/us to world-centric/all of us to Kosmos-centric/all-that-is perspectives. The respective work of Ken Wilber, Susanne Cook-Greuter, Robert Kegan, Bill Torbert, Don Beck and others offers examples of levels of consciousness.

Line of Development: Lines refer to developmental lines or multiple intelligences (Gardner). Integral Coaching uses six specific lines/intelligences: cognitive, moral, emotional, interpersonal, somatic, and spiritual. Over the course of the coaching relationship coaches leverage the stronger lines in order to help clients develop lines that need developing.

New Way of Being (NWOB): The NWOB suggests the expanded way in which the client will view the world, take action, and evaluate outcomes when he/she has successfully completed the coaching program. Each of us has a CWOB and we all grow into NWOB in repeated and ever widening cycles over our developmental lifetime. Integral Coaching builds the capacities and capabilities to grow into a NWOB while also working to integrate the healthy aspects of our CWOB as we transcend and include it.

Pathogenesis: The origination and development of a disease.

Quadrants: The Quadrants is a four-box matrix that maps four distinct perspectives on life. The Four Quadrants are:

1. **Upper left:** My beliefs and values—what and how I'm feeling or thinking right now—the interior of an individual, or intention
2. **Lower Left:** What we (you and I) believe or agree on—the interior of a collective, or culture
3. **Upper Right:** The observable aspects or exterior of an individual, or behavior, and

4. **Lower Right:** The observable aspects or exterior of a collective, or society.

Salutogenesis: The creation of health, or the fostering of healing.

Sense of Coherence: "The global orientation that expresses the extent to which an individual has a pervasive, enduring dynamic feeling of confidence that one's internal and external environments are predictable and that there is a high probability that things will work out as well as can reasonably be expected." (Antonovsky, 1979). The Sense of Coherence model includes three primary foci, comprehensibility, manageability, and meaning.

States of Consciousness: The quality of a client's energy affects how they engage in their topic, and working to shift those qualities can often help a client make and sustain notable shifts in their lives. States can refer to energetic shifts such as moods, as well as the larger realm of gross, subtle, causal, and non-dual states.

Type Structures: Types, refer to aspects of consciousness such as gender that exist at all developmental levels, but that do not, themselves, measure development—but within which development can take place. Examples include the Enneagram, Myers-Briggs, masculine/feminine, and ectomorphic/mesomorphic/endomorphic body types.

ABOUT THE AUTHORS

Joel Kreisberg, DC, ACC, is Executive Director of the Teleosis Institute—a nonprofit dedicated to Coaching and Narrative Healing. Through his 28 years of experience as an integrative physician, Joel has learned to recognize the healing potential in everyday actions and exchanges. Using natural systems, focused awareness, and fundamental life energy, he guides others to wholeness with greater resilience. Joel is an Integral Master Coach, an adjunct professor at Maryland University of Integrative Health, and he maintains a private practice Integrative Homeopathic Medicine in Berkeley, CA.

Alex Douds possesses more than 35 years of corporate experience in leadership roles. He has led teams in designing, developing, and evaluating award-winning human resources and leadership development programs that demonstrate positive return on investment with positive impacts on individual, team, and organizational performance. As a seasoned professional, he is a quick study on the barriers and challenges one faces in translating their vision and goals into reality. As an Integral Master Coach, he has a passion for coaching individuals in finding their own direction and self-expression and opening up to new possibilities and developing the skills needed to be the best they can be.

Julie Flaherty JD, is an attorney and Integral Master Coach. She provides counsel and coaching to clients ranging from nonprofits to Fortune 50 companies. She is the General Counsel for MATTER, a nonprofit on a mission to expand access to health care and food, both domestically and internationally. Julie is a graduate of the University of Minnesota and Integral Coaching Canada. As a result of her personal experience of being differently abled (as opposed to disabled), she has developed expertise in coaching clients through their journeys of healing. Julie is a leader of WEpractice, a relational, group-oriented practice that builds upon and transcends personal practice, allowing the development of skills in and the experience of an evolutionary collective field.

Karin Hempel is a seasoned technology executive working in the Financial Services industry. Her passion is working with others to enable them to reach their highest potential and have broad impact globally. Karin believes that technology can play a pivotal role in change—personal, group, and environmental. She has an MA in Holistic Health Education with a specialization in nutrition from John F. Kennedy University, and is a certified Integral Master Coach whose target clients are women undergoing transition as a result of life-altering events. Karin lives in Denver with her partner Tom and their two cats. Denver provides the perfect environment for Karin to indulge in her favorite activities of bicycling, hiking, and skiing.

Jill Lang Ward (1952-2016) has been an Integral Master Coach since 2006. Jill has helped many through transition, both professional and personal. Her experience as a cancer warrior since 2007 has deepened her insights, expanding her capacity to support others through life-altering circumstances. Since 2008, Jill has been actively involved with Myeloma Canada on regional and national advocacy initiatives including the Time to Live campaign. She offers peer support to patients and caregivers at the Algoma District Cancer Program, and is a Patient/Family Advisor with Cancer Care Ontario. Jill lives in Sault Ste. Marie, Ontario, along with husband Ted, Border Collie Brodie, and feline companion Bella. She enjoys meditation, journaling, reading, photography, and watercolour painting. Jill is fulfilling her lifelong dream of living on the majestic/mystical shores of Lake Superior where she finds peace … her personal place of healing.

Lois MacNaughton, BA, Integral Master Coach, ACC, is a life coach whose work combines Integral principles, Eastern philosophy, and a deep desire to reduce suffering in the world. She does this by helping individuals strengthen their resilience to deal with the ups and downs of life, to move out of reacting to responding to what is. She is certified in Deep Change's SQ21 and Integral Development's 360° LMP, and includes Integral Life Practice in her work. As a Reiki Master, Lois also brings healing energy to her coaching practice.

Reggie Marra, MA, ACC, engages coaching, poetry writing, humor, and any means necessary to help alleviate his own and others' unnecessary suffering. Author of three poetry and three nonfiction books, including the 2016 release, *And Now, Still,* Reggie serves as Creative Director at the Teleosis Institute. He is an Integral Master Coach, a Leadership Agility 360 Coach, and a mentor coach with the ICF, Integral Coaching Canada and Maryland University of Integrative health. He was his mom's primary caregiver for her final three-and-a-half years.

Amy Phillips is a business consultant and Integral Master Coach based in Vancouver, British Columbia. Her company, Aim True

Enterprises Inc., was founded in 2002 after a 10-year administrative career at the University of British Columbia. With a passion for creating healthy, welcoming environments and an intuitive ability to create order out of chaos, she found project management in the construction field a natural progression. And while she remains grateful to the many benefits this career Path has afforded her, it is all in service of a greater love—one of wellness—for herself, for others, for organizations, and for the planet. This love has inspired many diverse explorations, most recently ICC's certification program. At last the two begin to weave together as she focuses her talents on helping individuals and organizations uncover a deeper sense of wellbeing, inside and out.

John Stoddart, health coach, educator, advocate, and certified Integral Master Coach, is based in Ottawa and Vancouver, Canada. As a former filmmaker and TV producer, John made documentaries on disability rights, created Vancouver Film School's award-winning documentary program, and was director of their foundation film program and Capilano University's television studio. His unique approach to coaching and healing harnesses the power within his clients to develop optimum health, quality of life, and productivity. He is dedicated to the application and growth of health coaching within medicine and the healing arts.

Leslie Williams is a highly experienced leadership development professional who increases organizations' effectiveness by strengthening their leaders. Whether working as an executive coach, trainer, or facilitator, Leslie combines her in-depth understanding of systems and individuals to create meaningful and lasting change for her clients. She has served as Senior Faculty of Integral Coaching Canada, Inc., and as Adjunct Faculty of Georgetown University's Organization

Development Certificate Program. Leslie is a Master Certified Coach, which is the coaching profession's highest designation. She has a master's degree in Organization Development from American University/NTL Institute and a bachelor's degree in Music from Pomona College in Claremont, CA.

ABOUT INTEGRAL COACHING CANADA, INC.

Integral Coaching Canada, Inc., is a professional Integral Coaching® training company located in Ottawa, Canada. Founded by Master Certified Coaches Laura Divine and Joanne Hunt, ICC's proprietary Integral Coaching® adult development technology, coaching method, and coach training (Integral Coaching® Certification Program) are unequaled in the world. Integral Master Coach™ and Integral Coaching® are trademarks owned in Canada by Integral Coaching Canada, Inc. All references to Integral Master Coach™ and Integral Coaching® in this document refer to the Integral Coaching® method, process, and adult development technology developed and taught by Integral Coaching Canada, Inc.

CPSIA information can be obtained
at www.ICGtesting.com
Printed in the USA
BVHW031843180421
605140BV00001B/53

9 781495 187711